LANCASTER BOTTLES
GUIDES TO LANCASTER BOTTLE COLLECTING

Vol. 1
Lancaster, Pennsylvania
(Beers, Mineral Waters & Soft Drinks)

Edition limited to ~~500~~ copies,

of which this is number _____548_____

To Tim —
Happy Collecting!

Sam Nolt 6/7/14

Authors

John Long • Sam Nolt • Curt Tomlinson

Copyright ©2007 Lancaster Bottle Books, LLC.

All rights reserved. No part of this publication may be reproduced, stored in a retrieval system, or transmitted in any form or by any means electronic, mechanical, photocopying, recording or otherwise, without the prior written permission of the publisher.

Published by:

Lancaster Bottle Books, LLC.
P. O. Box 8763
Lancaster, PA 17604-8763

Library of Congress Catalog Number: 2007937266

International Standard Book Number (ISBN)
Paper: 978-1-4276-2616-5

Printed in the United States of America
1st Edition, by White Oak Printing Company
           Lancaster, PA

PREFACE

Many articles and books have been written on the subject of the various types of glass bottles. Rarely has one been written regarding those identifiable bottles relating to the brewing and bottling industry of a specific town or city.

The authors of this book believe that it would be exciting and rewarding to share their knowledge and collections by publishing a reference book identifying the majority of collectible bottles from the Lancaster, Pennsylvania brewing industry. The idea and need for this volume began nearly half a century ago. With the advent of modern printing methods and computer technology, the compilation and production of this book became a reality. It has taken nearly two years of actual researching, writing, organizing, and photographing of the many types and varieties of bottles used by the Lancaster brewers and bottlers. It is our sincere hope that our efforts prove of interest and value to our many collector friends.

For those readers who may not be collectors, we trust that the book will be appreciated as we have attempted to make it attractive and interesting from an historical perspective. Ours is a sincere effort to arrange, classify, and present in a simple and pictorial manner the available information that we have learned from our years of research, and from the assistance of our other collecting friends. The majority of our conclusions are specific facts while a few others are presumed.

Further study and research will likely reveal new facts, expand the knowledge that presently exists, and uncover additional information that will assist in our research.

We are honored to present this exciting publication, and we truly wish it to be of value to you as a collector.

The Authors

ACKNOWLEDGMENTS

This book has been the culmination of over forty years of research, collecting, documenting, and cataloging the history of the Lancaster, Pennsylvania brewing and bottling industries. The authors have spent over 2,000 hours during the making of this book. We have been blessed with the assistance of many of the following people who have willingly shared their knowledge, research, and collections:

- Todd Brubaker
- Jeff DeHart - (Conestoga Auction Company)
- Godfrey Engle
- Tom Fridy
- Doug Graham
- Don Haerter
- Jere Hambleton
- Merv Hemperly
- James Hosler
- Duff Lefever
- Rick Long
- Chris Raezer
- Walter Rowen -(Susquehanna Glass)
- Tod Von Mechow -(Philadelphia Bottle Book)
- Pat Zaephel
- Jay Buch
- Roy Duke, Jr.
- John Frantz - (Lancaster Brewing Co.)
- Todd Guion
- Don Hallacher
- Jere Hemperly
- Ken Hill
- Lancaster County Historical Society
- Steve Michaels
- Lloyd Reese
- Scott Sweger
- Josh Weirich
- Kerry Wetterstrom

We would also like to give special thanks to Eric Etkin, V.P., Seisan, LLC. for designing our research database and the www.lancasterbottlebooks.com website. Special thanks to Cortney Milbourne for layout and design.

To all of those persons mentioned above, and to our families and others who have helped us, we owe our heartfelt thanks for their patience, support, and guidence in the completion of this book.

Thank you,

John, Sam, and Curt

FOREWORD

Many of the early settlers of southeastern Pennsylvania, who came here in the 1600's through the 1800's, were of eastern European ancestry. They brought with them their religion, skills, and habits. Brewing was one of the skills that they were able to continue in this area.

As a result of this immigration to Lancaster, Pennsylvania, four major breweries evolved. These were Haefner, Reiker, Sprenger, and Wacker. Most of the beer produced in these breweries was sold in kegs, but some was marketed in bottles.

Lancaster, sometimes called the "Munich of the New World," was so named because of the good reputations of the brewers' quality and varieties of their beer.

Bottling, however, did not become prevalent until the 1870's. At first, the brew in the bottles was sealed with cork. This did not always provide a good gas seal. Later, rubber and ceramic stoppers were used as these could be fastened securely with wires. The bottle crown, or "cap," was invented in 1892, and it gradually replaced all other types of closures.

Bottle design changed over the years as new glass manufacturing technology evolved.

Each of the four major breweries had its own bottling department. However, many independent bottlers also set up business in Lancaster. Little did these bottlers realize that collectors today would battle with reckless abandon for a chance to own a "throw away" piece of glass with an unusual name on it.

The Authors

INTRODUCTION TO BOTTLE COLLECTING

Once you as a new enthusiast decide to become a serious collector, your quest for knowledge grows rapidly. Your search to acquire Lancaster items becomes a real challenge.

Unfortunately, researching this fascinating hobby is not easy. Very little written information of any type is available. It should be noted that the following suggestions are to be considered:
(1) concentrate on one area of collecting at a time, (2) purchase a specific item that is the best conditioned example, and (3) inexpensive items that are not perfect will soon have to be replaced at a later date.

We hope that this reference book provides the needed information for a novice or veteran collector, so as to provide a level playing field during your quest.

Whether you decide to collect Lancaster bottles, whiskey items, stoneware, ephemera, or any other advertising items, you will quickly learn that the following areas are where you should concentrate your efforts:

Family or Friends

Often learning of your interest, a family member or friend may possess an item that they would be more than happy to give you. This item may be something of little value or possibly a scarce or valuable piece.

Other Collectors

You, as a new Lancaster collector, will soon learn the names of the fellow collectors. Some will be quite elusive and ignore you; others will be just the opposite, and will be excited to share any information they possess. Also, they usually offer to sell any duplicate items. This is very good as it provides you, as a new collector, with fairly accurate pricing information on a specific item and may lead to an exciting friendship.

Flea Markets and Yard Sales

Knowledge of these areas quite often results in obtaining a new item for your collection. Sometimes, the seller has no idea whether the asking price is too low, fair, or completely out of line. This can be good and bad. If you are lucky, you can purchase the item at a fair price. However, as an uneducated collector, it is possible to pay far too much. This has to be taken into consideration when first starting to collect and is definitely part of the learning curve.

As veteran collectors will point out, "You always remember those items that you paid too much for, but you forget the items you located at a very inexpensive price or were given."

Antique Shops and Shows

Many Lancaster collectors routinely visit the various shops, co-ops, or shows in the Lancaster area and surrounding vicinities. We are blessed to have locations such as Renningers, Black Angus, Shupps Grove, Adams, and many other desirable shops in the Adamstown, Pennsylvania area. This "hot bed of collecting" has often been referred to as the "antique capital of the US."

Introduction to Bottle Collecting - Continued

Auctions

Many veteran Lancaster collectors decide to sell their duplicates or their entire collections at auction. We are very fortunate to have several first class auction houses in the Lancaster area. Conestoga Auction Company is one of the premier companies to offer this service. Other first class companies are Eric Probst Auction Company and Horst Auction Company. Of course, there are several other excellent auction companies that occasionally offer Lancaster collectibles for sale.

Ebay

Almost every day, many Lancaster collectors scan the thousands of items offered on Ebay. This can be very rewarding as new items turn up regularly. Of course, the bidding is usually quite competitive between collectors.

Digging and Dumps

New collectors learn that "hidden treasures" can be found buried in the ground. In the Lancaster area there is a select group of collectors who have demonstrated a passion for digging.

They first concentrated their efforts on old dumping grounds, ravines, wooded areas, sink holes, old barns, and buildings. They learned the possibility of greater success was in old privies (outhouses), wells, and cisterns.

It is obvious that in the old days, household trash was not collected as it is today. Therefore, each person or household had to dispose of unwanted items the best way they could. This was especially difficult if they lived in the city. The outhouse presented the opportune method to dispose of unwanted items, especially bottles.

When permission was given, digging took place in the backyard where old outhouses had been located by slight depressions, discolorations, or probe use. If the homeowner was not wealthy, he could not afford to have the outhouse "dipped" or cleaned. The average "undipped" outhouse usually lasted about 20 years. As an outhouse pit filled, a new pit was dug and the outhouse was relocated. Thus, backyards may contain five or more outhouse pits of different ages. The pits usually reflect the following ages: pontil, smooth base soda, blob, hutch, crown top and milk.

It is not unusual for these professional diggers to dig down 15 feet to 25 feet to hopefully locate a buried treasure. This is extremely dangerous and should never be attempted by a novice.

The best advice is to find out who the professional diggers are and if possible "watch them in action." You will quickly learn that most of the time there are many hours spent with nothing to show for it. However, as one avid digger once said, "There is always the next hole!"

THE FOUR MAJOR LANCASTER BREWERIES

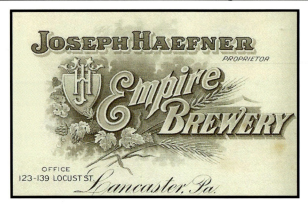

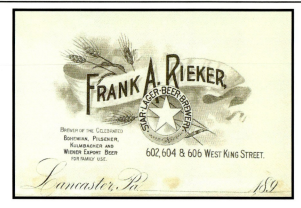

Haefner Brewery   **Rieker Star Brewery**

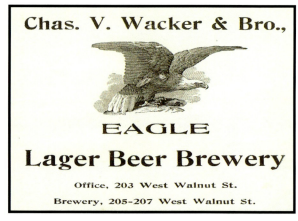

Sprenger Brewery   **Wacker Brewery**

FAMOUS LANCASTER BEER BARONS

John A. Sprenger
First formed his own brewery with his brother Jacob J. in 1852. By 1884, he owned the largest brewery in Lancaster. Named the "Excelsior Brewery," it was Lancaster's finest until the Rieker Brewery was completed in the mid 1890's.

Joseph Haefner
After working for several breweries, he purchased the Lawrence Knapp "Empire Brewery" in 1886. When Joseph died in 1893, his sons ran the brewery until 1945. It closed when they could no longer compete with larger, modern breweries.

Charles V. Wacker
Son of Joseph Wacker, along with his brother Joseph, Jr., operated the brewery from 1880 until 1938. It was known as "Charles V. Wacker and Bros." The family interest ceased, and for three years it operated as the "Old Lancaster Brewing Company." In 1942, until closing in 1956, it reverted back to the "Wacker Brewing Co."

Frank A. Rieker
Owner and proprietor of Lancaster's largest and finest brewery. Always sensitive to the taste of the beer-drinking public, Frank proclaimed that his beer was far superior to all others. He died on August 4, 1907.

John G. Forstberg
Much of the phenomenal success of the Rieker Star Brewery is probably attributed to the brilliant supervision of John Forstberg. He was plant supervisor from 1891 until 1898. He was the "most important person in Rieker's entire brewing operation."

Frank J. Rieker
He was the son of Frank A. and, like his father, was civic-minded. He ran for mayor of Lancaster in 1904 but was unsuccessful. Frank J. ran the brewery after his father died, until it closed in 1941.

HISTORY OF THE FOUR MAJOR BREWERIES

Haefner Brewing Co.

Joseph Haefner was born in Germany in September 1852. He moved to America in 1872 where he worked for various breweries. His father, Joseph Haefner, Sr., was a prominent brewer in Germany. Young Joseph learned the art of brewing from his father, and in 1875, he moved to the Pennsylvania area and worked in Philadelphia, Pottsville, and Reading.

In 1886, he met Lawrence Knapp in Lancaster, and then purchased the Lawrence Knapp "Empire Brewery," which was located at Lime and Locust Streets. The Knapp Brewery was one of Lancaster's oldest breweries and dated back to 1868.

In 1874, Joseph married Raphel Fisher's daughter Margaret, and they had seven children. None of these children were involved in their father's business. However, Joseph did adopt another son named Henry Charles Haefner, who was commonly called "Harry." Harry and his brother-in-law, Isaac B. Powl, took over the daily operation of the brewery in 1916 when Joseph died. These two gentlemen continued to run the brewery until it ceased operation in 1945. During this time Harry and his wife had seven children. Five of these children worked at the brewery in one form or another. The Haefner family was quite prosperous and was recognized as one of Lancaster's finest.

Rieker Star Brewery

Frank A. Rieker was born in Wurttemberg, Germany on March 10, 1844. He decided to move to America in 1863 and worked in New York City and Philadelphia. On December 20, 1882, he purchased his first business in New York City. He paid $1,100 to Tillie Boelwiler for a confectionary candy and ice cream business located at 69 Sixth Ave. He continued to run this business for several years.

Frank then moved to Lancaster and planned to build his own brewery. This dream was realized when it took from 1892 to 1898 to erect a brewery complex at 602 West King Street. It was located on the site now known as Crystal Park. The brewery saloon along West King Street was called the Western Market Hotel. It later became Kirchner's Hotel, Lazuse's Bar, and is now known as the Blue Star Hotel.

On December 26, 1891, Frank A. Rieker made perhaps his most important decision when he hired John G. Forstberg as his brewery superintendent. His employment was to begin on January 15, 1892, for a period of one year. Forstberg was paid $3,000 a year and was to assume all responsibilities for the building of the brewery and the daily beer-making operations. Forstberg was granted a bonus of $25 for every 1,000 barrels of beer sold over the amounts sold from the first day of January 1891 to the first day of January 1892, the base year. On January 30, 1893, it was confirmed that 14,866 barrels were sold during the base year. The second year 18,303 barrels were sold. This was a net gain of 3,437 barrels and Forstberg received a bonus of $85.90. There is no doubt that John Forstberg made Frank A. Rieker a very wealthy man.

Frank A. Rieker married Cressentia Harmann in 1868, and they had six children. He died on August 4, 1907. Two years before his death in 1905 he built a large home located on Marietta Avenue at the corner of Race Avenue. He contracted with Jacob Stumpf to build his house for $12,990.

History of the Breweries - Continued

When Frank A. died, the management of the brewery was taken over by his son Frank J. Rieker, who was very active in the Lancaster community. In 1904, he was the Democratic Party candidate for mayor and he lost the election. Frank J. was married twice and had two daughters and two sons. None of his children were involved in the family business. Frank J. died on August 9, 1944, after owning the brewery for many years. During prohibition, from 1918 until 1933, the Rieker family engaged in several businesses. The most important was called the Lancaster Security Real Estate Company. This company leased the brewing operation to outside interests. After the repeal of prohibition, an attempt was made to resume the brewing operation. The name was changed to the Penn Star Brewery and finally the Penn State Brewery (formerly Riekers). This final attempt lasted from 1934 to 1936. The brewery ceased operations at that time and was finally demolished in1941.

An interesting aside was that during Prohibition Lancaster, being "the brewing capital of Pennsylvania," was subject to a number of raids by police and federal agents on local "bootleggers," (makers of illegal beer and alcoholic beverages). An interesting story about one of these raids was first reported in a Lancaster newspaper on March 16, 1932. A city employee, while repairing a sewer, discovered a rubber brewer's hose in the sewer at the intersection of West King and Pine streets. Upon investigation by police, it was reported that a hose ran about four city blocks from Rieker's Brewery down King Street to Water Street. At Water Street it ran north under West Orange Street to a vacant building at 112 North Water Street. The line had been run through the sewers by dwarfs hired in New Jersey. Some of the sewer lines were only 18" in diameter.

J. A. Sprenger

The name Sprenger represents one of the earliest family names of brewers in Lancaster. Abraham Sprenger was born in Rheinfalz, Bavaria on July 5, 1770, and came to America at the age of 51 in 1821. He started his first brewery business in Maytown, PA for two years from 1829 to 1831. Next, he rented a brewery in 1836 from his brother-in-law John Borell. Abraham was stricken ill in 1843 at the age of 73, and his wife managed the business during his illness. Abraham died in 1854 at the age of 84.

His son, John Abraham Sprenger (J.A.), was born in Reading, PA in 1829 and was working in his father's establishment at the age of 10. In 1852, young J.A. joined into a partnership with his older brother, John Jacob Sprenger (J.J.). The joint venture lasted only 18 months. Hence, very few J.J. & J.A. Sprenger bottles are known.

In 1854, J.A. decided to go into business for himself. He leased what later became the Wacker Brewery. Then in 1857 he erected a new brewery and saloon at 125-127 East King Street. He operated this business at this location until 1873. Later, he leased a property on South Lime and Locust streets from Philip Frank who supplied malt. J.A. then purchased the brewery in 1883 and rebuilt and enlarged it. J.A. named the new large facility the "Excelsior Brewery." In November 1896, J.A. sold the brewery to a new corporation who changed the name back to the Sprenger Brewing Company.

It is very interesting that there are no bottles known during the period that Abraham Sprenger and his wife ran the brewery (from 1836 to 1867). Also, during the early years of J.A.'s brewing career from 1854 to 1883 no known bottles exist. Further research is needed to explain the lack of Abraham and J.A. Sprenger bottles during the years 1836 to 1883.

History of the Breweries - Continued

J.J. Sprenger

John Jacob Sprenger was born January 1, 1825, in Reading, PA. He moved to Lancaster with his parents in 1836 at the age of 11. He attended public schools in Lancaster and, upon graduation, learned the family trade of brewing.

He then went into the bottling business in Blair County and returned to Lancaster in 1852, when he engaged in a partnership with his younger brother John Abraham (J.A.). This partnership lasted only 18 short months.

J.J. lived in Europe from 1857 to 1862 and returned to Lancaster to purchase his father's brewery at Walnut and Water streets. He ran this operation for several years. J.J. loved to travel and, during the next 20 years, made three more trips to Europe. When he finally returned to the United States, he settled in Georgia. He ran another bottling business in Rome and then in Atlanta. J.J. Sprenger was a very enterprising man. He traveled extensively, excelled as a writer, and had above average intellectual skills. He died on December 2, 1902.

J.J. & J.A. Sprenger

J.J. Sprenger was born January 1, 1825 and his younger brother J.A. Sprenger was born January 26, 1829. These brothers came from a family of brewers that represented one of the earliest in Lancaster. Although they were involved in this business their entire lives, the brothers formed a partnership which lasted only 18 months (from 1852 until 1854).

Sprenger Brewing Company

In November 1896, J.A. Sprenger sold his brewery to a corporation which continued the Sprenger Brewing Company name. Ferdinand Grebe, Frederick Waller, and Paul Heine, Sr. ran the business and, in 1905, they remodeled and enlarged their complete operation. With the advent of prohibition in 1918, the brewery converted to the manufacturing of cereal beverages. Although they produced as many as 60,000 barrels of beer annually prior to prohibition, they were not as successful when prohibition ended in 1933. In approximately 1926, John Duschl and William F. Dirian took over leadership of the plant. However, Duschl left sometime later and Dirian remained. In 1948, Guy Eckman and James Sullenberger joined Dirian as owners. By 1951, the old equipment became obsolete and the plant could no longer compete with the larger facilities. By 1953, the plant closed forever.

Sprenger Bottler

When J.A. Sprenger sold the brewery to a corporation in November of 1896, they continued the Sprenger Brewing Company name. However, examination of various bottles that were used during this time period suggests that some bottles also referred to the company as "Sprenger Bottler." The authors have decided to list these bottles under a separate category, even though they were produced and sold by the same Brewery.

History of the Breweries - Continued

Joseph Wacker Brewery

Joseph Wacker was born in Wurttemberg, Germany on December 23, 1830. He immigrated to America at the age of 19. He first tried to become a baker which lasted only a short time. Next, he worked as a hired hand on several local farms. He learned the art of brewing three years later at John Wittlinger's Brewery. He went to work for the Sprenger Bottling Works in 1854 and, shortly thereafter, he and George A. Kiehl purchased the company and called it "Kiehl and Wacker." It was located at 77 East King Street. In 1865, Joseph decided to go into business for himself and purchased the old Wittlinger brewery where he had worked earlier. He sold this business in 1868, which was actually in exchange for the County Hotel. In 1870, he bought the Eagle Brewery at 223 West Walnut Street from Jacob Sprenger. Joseph decided to retire in 1880 and turned the ownership over to his two sons, Charles V. Wacker and Joseph Wacker, Jr. Their business was known as the Wacker Bros. Brewery. Joseph Wacker, Sr. died on November 26, 1912. He was married to Mary Dettlinger and they had a total of six children.

Wacker Bros. Brewery

As stated before, Joseph Wacker turned the brewery over to his two sons in 1880. In 1894, the brewery at 223 West Walnut Street was destroyed by fire. It was rebuilt very quickly and made much larger and more modern. Charles V. and his brother Joseph Jr. continued this operation all during prohibition and finally retired in 1938 with the sale of the business.

It is reported that they paid the watchmen in the tower of the railroad at Walnut and Prince streets to warn them about police in the area.

Olde Lancaster Brewing Company

Following the end of Prohibition in 1938, the Wacker Brothers Brewing Company became known as the "Olde Lancaster Brewing Company." This operation only lasted for a period of three years. From 1942 to its closing in 1956, it reverted back to the Wacker Brewing Co. name.

Wacker Brewing Company

In 1942, the Olde Lancaster Brewing Company ceased operation, and the company was renamed Wacker Brewing Co. and resumed operation under new proprietorship. The Wacker family was no longer involved, as the brewery was owned by John Duschl and his son-in-law Paul Danz. These gentlemen ran the operation until it closed for good in 1956. They could no longer compete with the more modern operations. Wacker beer was the last of the original four major breweries to be sold in Lancaster County.

NOTE: As prohibition lasted from 1918 until 1933, no brewery or bottler was legally in operation. Please take note of this when dates are referenced in this book.

BOTTLE IDENTIFICATION

The first step in determining the value of a bottle is to identify the type of bottle. There are many aspects to bottle identification including shape, type of top, type of bottom, embossing, label, and color. The information below has been provided as a reference to assist in the identification process.

VARIANTS

Variations in bottles are one of the most misunderstood aspects of bottle collecting. But a variation in a bottle is just what bottle collectors always look for. The more unique or closer to a one of a kind variant, the more desirable the bottle becomes.

Variations consist of the following: color, size, shape, type top, type bottom, writing and most importantly the "slug plate" (embossing on the front of the bottle). The embossing is most often the most difficult element of a variation. The most desirable type of embossing is a mistake, such as Lancaster misspelled "Lancasater" or J & H Casper misspelled as "J & N Casper." As with other types of collectibles, mistakes can be very desirable.

Other types of embossing variations are very subtle, such as the word "Registered" above the slug plate versus below the slug plate. The words "This Bottle Not To Be Sold" can be found on the back of the bottle or the front of the bottle. Also, many times the actual slug plate is completely different. Larger or smaller letters, different styles of letters, horseshoes, monograms, curved lettering, straight lettering, and vertical lettering are examples of variants.

One of the least common known types of variant comes from the lack of customer service during the early years of bottle manufacturing. During the 1800's to early 1900's, it was a "buyer beware" type of manufacturing process. Unlike the excellent customer service of today, when a box of bottles arrived by stage coach or rail line, the customer simply accepted what was in the box. Of utmost importance regarding this factor was the beginning and ending of bottle runs at the bottle manufacturing facilities. Typically, the manufacturer would determine the number of bottles to be blown based on the color of glass that was currently in the furnace. Many times they would either run out of glass or have glass left over. Unlike today, this glass was simply used for the next run. As an example, it did not matter that the current color was aqua glass and the next run of bottles was amber. The manufacturer simply started the batch with the old glass and then switched to the new batch of glass. Often this created a one or two-of-a-kind variant in a unique color. This resulted in a very common bottle that could be found in a very unique color.

COLORS

Colors of bottles can vary greatly from honey amber, aqua, to almost opaque (sometimes referred to as black glass). Most variations were a result of the desires of the bottlers to either enhance the look of the product or to make their product saleable. Some variations are the direct result of low quality control standards during the nineteenth century. Many variations resulted from end-of-run glass changes, such as going from an amber batch to a clear batch. The last bottles produced would have become lighter in color, and the customer simply accepted the product. There are some very common variants that come in a unique color because either the current glass ran out or a new batch of bottles was created with the glass left over from the previous run. To help you better identify bottles we have supplied the color chart below.

Bottle Identification - Continued
COLOR CHART

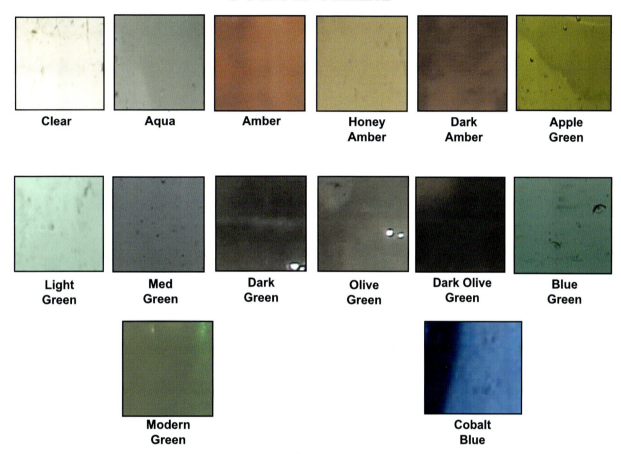

Clear	Aqua	Amber	Honey Amber	Dark Amber	Apple Green
Light Green	Med Green	Dark Green	Olive Green	Dark Olive Green	Blue Green
Modern Green			Cobalt Blue		

Blob Top

The blob top bottle is one of the most common types of bottle known, mostly due to the ease of production and the success of the wire bail enclosure. Most blob top bottles come in two types: the tall blob (approximately 9.00" to 9.75") and the small blob (approximately 6.00" to 7.75").

Tall Blob

Small Blob

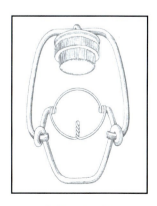

Wire Bail

Bottle Identification - Continued

Squats

The squat type of bottle was the earliest form of bottle produced. Most have either a Double-Tapered Applied Top or Single-Taper Applied Top. Most squats come in shades of green ranging from light aqua to almost black glass in color. Our extensive research has identified only a few examples of extremely rare cobalt blue Lancaster squat bottles. Most squats were cork sealed with a cork and wire bail covering. These bottles had either an iron pontil or smooth base finish. This early type bottle was used for beer, mineral water, and soda.

Squat with an Applied Top

Squat with an Double Taper Top

Hutchs (Hutchinsons)

Charles G. Hutchinson, the son of a prominent Chicago bottler, invented on April 8, 1879, the most popular of the internal stoppers that replaced the cork closure on blob-top soda bottles. He named his invention the "Hutchinson Stopper." This invention heralded the beginning of a new bottle - the Hutchinson-stoppered bottle. The stopper consisted of a rubber gasket (which came in five sizes to accommodate neck diameters) held between two metal plates and attached to a spring wire stem (which came in three sizes to accommodate neck lengths). A portion of the looped wire stem protruded above the mouth of the bottle, while the lower end with the gasket and plates extended far enough into the bottle to allow the gasket to fall below the neck.

To seal the bottle after it had been filled, the rubber disk was pulled by the wire stem. The bottle was then inverted and righted. This motion formed the seal and the pressure of the carbonation forced the rubber gasket to remain against the shoulder of the bottle.

A very unusual container to say the least, the Hutchinson-stoppered bottle (and its several imitators) enjoyed great popularity during the closing years of the nineteenth century. By 1890, W. H. Hutchinson & Son claimed a customer list of over three thousand and reported that their price of $2 to $2.50 per gross was more than competitive.

Bottle Identification - Continued

Hutchs (Hutchinsons) - Continued

By 1912, the adoption of the crown cork was so widespread that the largest manufacturer and originator of the Hutchinson-type stopper, W. H. Hutchinson & Son of Chicago, ceased production. As late as the 1920's, Hutchinson-stoppered bottles were being used by some small American companies, but shortly thereafter all states adopted laws restricting the use of internal stoppered bottles on the basis that they were unsanitary.

Hutch or Hutchinson

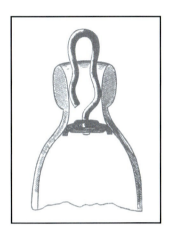

Hutch with wire stopper

Gravitating Stopper

These bottles are differentiated by having internal stopper closures (i.e. not cork sealed) and often body and/or finish shapes that were designed to accommodate these unique closures. Both of the major covered styles have long, moderate diameter bodies, short to non-existent necks, and are topped with some variation of the blob finish. These were the Gravitating Stopper and Hutchinson Spring Stopper styles. The Hutchinson type was the more popular of these two styles, though both stopper types could apparently be used on the other style of bottle. The Codd style bottle is also technically an internal stopper type but is covered separately in this section. The Gravitating Stopper was produced for a very short time, as it was outlawed for unsanitary reasons. When it was opened, the tapered glass stopper fell into the product.

Bottle Identification - Continued

Gravitating Stopper

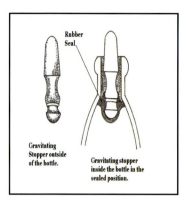

Gravitating Stopper with Glass stopper

Codd's Ball Stopper

The Codd's ball stopper soda water (rarely beer) bottle style was by far the most successful of an assortment of internal ball type stoppers for soda bottles devised during the second half of the 19th century. It was first patented in 1870 in England, with patents for the most commonly seen types granted in 1872 and 1873. It was introduced in the United States in 1873. Most of its success was in England or in the Commonwealth nations like Canada, India, and Australia. Similar to the round bottom sodas, this closure and bottle style was infrequently used by American soda bottlers (primarily due to the fierce competition from the Hutchinson and later crown closures). It may never have actually been produced in this country. George A. Kiehl was the only Lancaster bottler to use this type of enclosure. Three variations of this type of bottle exist.

Codd's Ball - Side View

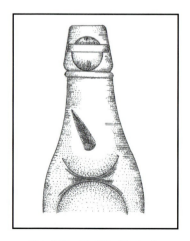

Codd's Ball - Front View

Bottle Identification - Continued
Three-Piece Mold

In conjunction with the true two-piece mold, one of the earliest mold types to be used in the U.S. was the "three-piece mold," originally patented by H. Ricketts (Bristol, England) in 1821, and likely adapted into the U.S. by the 1830's (McKearin & Wilson 1978). Although earlier versions of a three-piece mold may pre-date the Ricketts' mold, it is not certain. If so, they would have been essentially a dip mold with two shoulder mold sections added.

Morphologically, typical three-piece mold bottles have a horizontal mold seam encircling the bottle where the shoulder and body meet, and two mold seams on opposite sides running vertically from the shoulder seam, up the shoulder, and variably up the neck and/or finish. The picture below of a light amethyst liquor bottle shows a close-up of the very distinct mold seams on the shoulder and neck of this later mouth-blown, three-piece mold liquor bottle dating from the early 20th century (1900-1910). Consider the location of the mold seams in the picture with the conformation of the three-piece mold in the illustration below. Three-piece mold liquor bottles were a popular style and manufacturing method into the early 20th century and are shown in catalogs dating until at least 1908 (Illinois Glass Co. 1908).

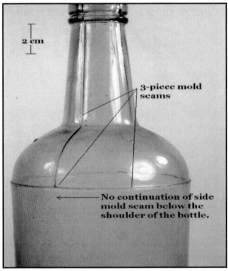

Three-piece mold bottle

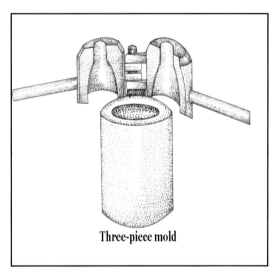

Actual three-piece mold

Pony Bottle

The Pony bottle refers to its small size, often referred to as a small beverage bottle, holding approximately seven ounces of beverage. Many Pony bottles were sold by the half dozen (known as a six pack today) or by the dozen.

Bottle Identification - Continued

Pony Bottles

Crown Top

The typical crown top finish is usually two-parts being comprised of a rounded narrow "bead" upper part (also called a "locking ring" or "locking bead"), which actually holds the cap on top of a variably rounded or flattened lower part that varies widely in height and conformation (Anonymous 1929; Lief 1965). The only consistent feature between the many variations of the crown top accepting finishes was the bead upper part or lip, which was 1" (~2.5 cm) in diameter and continues to be the diameter today over 100 years later.

Tall vs. Small Crown Soda Old   **Tall vs. Small Crown Soda Modern**

Type Bottoms

Typically the base of a bottle has one primary function, besides helping to hold the bottle together, and that is to provide a flat surface for the bottle to stand upright. "Flat" bottle bottoms are never

Bottle Identification - Continued

totally flat, but instead are usually indented or domed upwards. Why? The following is from the British Glass website "Glasspac" and explains it, at least in part:

"Bottle bottoms aren't flat because they need an arched structure to allow them to be stable on a flat surface. The bottom of a bottle is usually the thickest part, retaining more temperature throughout the production line. Because the bottom is hotter, it is also more fluid and has a tendency to sag, forming a shape like a spinning top which makes it unstable on flat surfaces. Giving a bottle an arched shape at the bottom means that, if it does sag, it can do so without touching the bottom."

In conjunction with the finish (lip), the various attributes and features found on the base of a bottle allow for some of the better opportunities for the manufacturing-based dating of a bottle. There are four basic bottom types in Lancaster, PA bottles. The types are shown by age: Iron Pontil or Sand Pontil, Smooth Base with no bottler identification marks, and Smooth Base with bottler identification marks.

Iron Pontil - Notice Residue

Sand Pontil - No Residue

Smooth Base, squat soda no bottler marks

Smooth Base - Bottler Marks are Common

Type Tops

Lancaster City bottles in this book have four basic top types. They are the Double-Taper Applied Top, Applied Top, Blob Top and Crown Top. The oldest of these are the Double-Taper Applied Top and the Applied Top. The first two types are basically the same in that the bottle was blown in a mold that consisted of the body, shoulder and a portion of the neck. After the bottle was blown it

Bottle Identification - Continued

was placed on the pontil rod that either consisted of heated glass attached to the base of the bottle, or an iron rod that was attached to the base of the bottle. While the bottle was on the pontil rod, an amount of molten glass was applied to the end of the neck and a lipping tool was used to finish the top. It is the lipping tool and the skill of the glass blower that determines Double-Taper from simply an applied top. The transition from applied tops to tooled tops to molded tops occurred from approximately 1850 until 1890, with smaller bottles like medicines completing the transition by the 1870's. As the glass-making process progressed, glass makers became more skilled, and the quality of glass improved, so entire bottles could be made and blown in the mold. Also, with the introduction of the snap-case holder there was no further need for the pontil rod, so most bottles became totally smooth-based during the 1870's and 1880's. It was during this time that the blob top became very popular with the introduction of the enclosed metal stopper, pasteurization, and enhanced transportation capabilities. Also, during the late 1880's to early 1890's, early crown top bottles and enclosures began to appear. Early crown bottles are often mistaken for machine-made bottles. However, this was not always the case. By the early 20th century, machine-type bottle-making capabilities had improved and crown bottles became the norm.

Double-Taper Applied Top

Applied Top

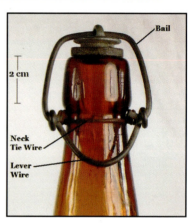

Blob Top

Crown Top

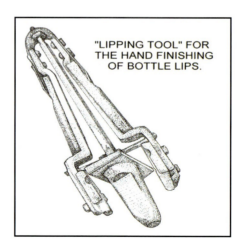

"LIPPING TOOL" FOR THE HAND FINISHING OF BOTTLE LIPS.

Some of the text and illustrations are courtesy of the **Historic Glass Bottle Identification & Information Website**, with permission from William Lindsey, http://bottleinfo.historicbottles.com. This has been an invaluable resource, a must for all bottle collectors.

List of Bottlers

1. Bair, John F.
2. Bair & Groff
3. Beaver Bottling Works
4. Bertl, Louis
5. Bryden, A. M.
6. C. G. & Co.
   Caspar J&H (misspelled - a for e)
7. Casper, John
8. Casper, J. & H.
9. Casper, J. & N. (misspelled – N for H)
10. Chamberlin, W.C.
    Chuk-ker Beverages of Lanc., see Dr Pepper
11. Coca-Cola, Lancaster
12. Coldren, John L.
13. Conestoga Bottling Works
14. Copland, Jacob
15. Crystal Rock Beverage Co.
16. Diehl, F. C. (son)
17. Diehl, P. P. (father)
18. Dr. Pepper Bottling Co.
19. Duke, Roy
20. Eagle Bottling Works
21. East End Bottling Works
22. Empire Bottling Works
23. Empire Bottling Works, Joseph Haefner
    Engel Bottling Works, Fred, (Engel for Engle)
24. Engle, F.
25. Engle Bottling Works, The Fred
26. Engle Bottling Works, 'D'
27. Enterprise Bottling Supply Co. of PA
28. Frey, W. B.
29. Fulmer, A. P. (paper label)
30. Gerstly, W. F.
31. Gibson, L. L.
    G/R - See George E. Reese
32. Grimecy, Harry W.
33. H. L. F. & Co.
34. Haefner Brewing Co.
35. Hain, Charles
36. Hallman, H. C.
37. Hambright W. A.
    Hanbright, W. A. (misspelled n for m)
38. Haus, B. F.
39. Hygrade Bottling Works
40. Ingleside Bottling Works
    J/S - See J. Schwende
41. Keefer, W. W.
42. Kegel, H. J.
43. Kiehl, George A.
44. Kiehl & Keefer
45. Kiehl & Keefer/Schlitz
46. Kiehl & Wacker
47. Kist Bottling Co.
58. Klugh, Adam M.
49. Krimmel, August
50. Lancaster Bottling Co C.G. Bates&Son Mgrs.
51. Lancaster Bottling Co.
52. Lancaster Bottling Works
53. Lancaster Brewery, Inc. (old)
54. Lancaster Brewing, Co. (modern)
56. Lancaster Malt Brewing, Co.
56. McGrann, Michael
57. Metropolitan Bottling Works
58. Metzger Bros.
59. Mil-Co
60. Miller, Philip H.
61. Nehi Bottling Co.
62. Norbeck, Geo. S.
63. Olde Lancaster Brewing Co.
64. Penn Star Brewery
65. Penn State Brewery
66. Pontz, John
67. Pure Beverage Co.
68. Quade, F.
69. Reese, George E.
70. Rieker, Frank A.
71. Ruttgers Weiss Bier, C.
72. Schaeffer, A. B.
73. Schmidt & Co., J.
74. Schmitt & Beilman
75. Schwende, J.
76. Seven Up Bottling Co. (sno-maid)
77. Shadel
78. Sprenger Bottler
79. Sprenger Brewing Co.
80. Sprenger Company, The
81. Sprenger, E. E.
82. Sprenger, G. F.
83. Sprenger, J. A.
84. Sprenger, J. J.
85. Sprenger, J. J. & J. A.
    Springer, E. E. (misspelled i for e)
86. Springer, Nelson H.
87. Star Bottling Company
88. Star Bottling Works
89. Star Brewing & Bottling Co.
    Suncrest Bottling Company, see Dr. Pepper
90. Todd, Harry
91. Tretter, John N.
92. Tretter and Son
93. Ulmer, H. W.
94. Wacker Brewing Co.
95. Wacker Bros.
96. Wacker, Joseph
97. Walker, Thomas
98. Wall, George
99. Wanbaugh & Haines
100. Ware, E. C. (Ware Bottling Enterprise)
101. Weber, George
102. Whistle Bottling Co.
103. Wiley, Myers E.
104. Wolpert, Peter K.
105. Zech, Charles
     Zeck, Charles (misspelled)

Map of Lancaster

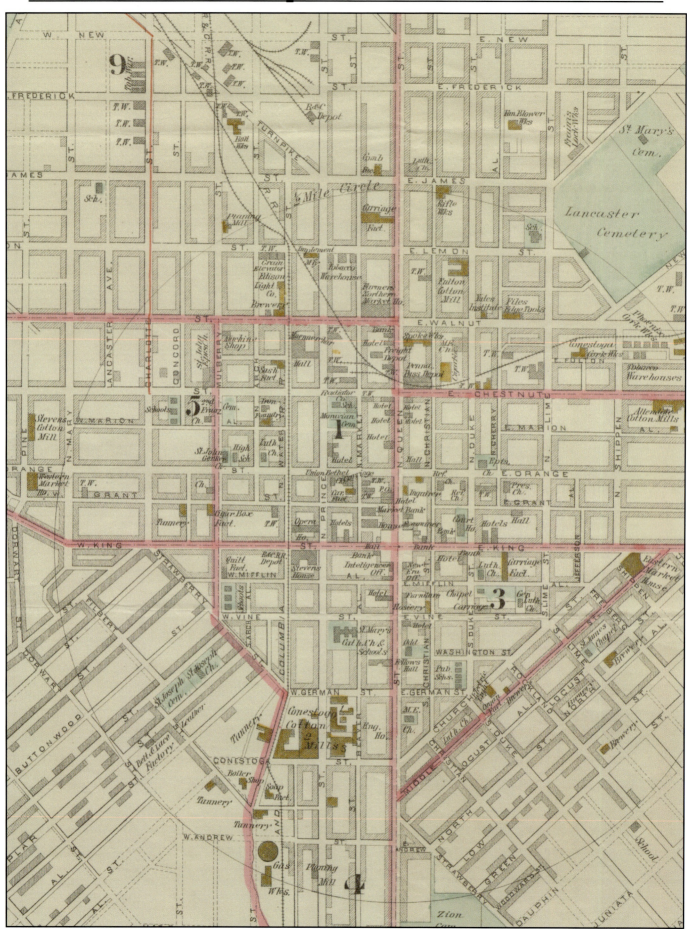

Biographies

BAIR, JOHN F.
1898 - 1916 - BOTTLER

Bus: 31 South Lime Street

Res: 24 North Broad Street

Products: Beer, Ale, Porter, Mineral Water, Koca-Nola, Ballentines Sparkling Ale

Facts: Address same as George F. Sprenger, E.E. Sprenger and misspelled E.E. Springer

BAIR & GROFF
1897 - BOTTLERS

Bus: 31 South Lime Street

Facts: Business address same as John F. Bair, George F. Sprenger, E.E. Sprenger and misspelled E.E. Springer. Oscar Groff was a "Silent Partner."

BEAVER BOTTLING WORKS
1920 - 1930 (APPROX.) - BOTTLER

Facts: Authors believe this bottle has some relationship to Roy E. Duke and/or P. P. Diehl at 21 West Farnum Street. Very similar slug plate to Eagle Bottling Works.

BERTL, LOUIS
BOTTLER

Facts: Extensive research of all Lancaster City and County records has failed to find any information on this bottler. In fact, the name Bertl is not listed in any city directory. The style of bottles known suggests a time period of 1900 - 1910.

BRYDEN, A. M.
1879 - 1880 - BOTTLER

Bus: 257 West King Street

Products: Beer, Ale

Facts: Also worked in Hazleton, PA and Wilkes Barre, PA. Those bottles are also available.

C. G. & CO. (CHARLES GROVE)
1870'S - BOTTLER

Bus: Address not known, although 15 Penn Square was listed as his address for his liquor and wine business.

Facts: Best known for liquor bottles with one type of beer bottle known in two variants.

CASPAR, J&H (JOHN & HENRY)
1859 - 1876 - BOTTLER

Facts: Please see J&H Casper below, misspelled Caspar, should be Casper.

CASPER, J. (JOHN)
1863 - 1876 - BOTTLER

Bus: 59 South Queen Street

Products: Lemon and Sarsaparilla Mineral Waters and others

CASPER, J&H (JOHN & HENRY)
1859 - 1876 - BOTTLER

Bus: South Mulberry Street, opposite school house, 1859 - 1860; 59 South Queen Street, 1861 - 1876

Products: Lemon and Sarsaparilla Mineral Water and others

CASPER, J&N
1859 - 1876

Facts: Please see J&H Casper above, misspelled J&N, should be J&H.

CHAMBERLIN, W. C. (WILLIAM)
1853 - 1860 - BOTTLER

Bus: King & Mulberry, listed as near Water Street

Res: 84 West King Street. Wife Mary lived at 257 West King Street after William's death.

Biographies - Continued

Facts: William died in 1857. Wife Mary F. ran the business until 1860. This is the earliest known Lancaster dark green squat.

CHUK-KER BOTTLING WORKS
BOTTLER

Facts: There is no information available to believe that there was ever a company called Chuk-ker Bottling Works operating in Lancaster. The authors believe this bottle was really a Dr. Pepper bottle labeled Chuk-ker Bottling Works. The Chuk-ker name was marketed and sold nationwide under various distributors. See Dr. Pepper.

COCA-COLA BOTTLING WORKS
1920 - 1971 - BOTTLER - DISTRIBUTOR

Bus: 417 East Ross Street; 551-553 Spruce Street

Products: Exclusive bottler of Coca Cola, Cherry Blossoms, True Fruit Grape and Crass

Facts: D. M. Sanderson, president; J. R. Shaw, manager.

COLDREN, JOHN L.
1900 - 1910 - BOTTLER

Bus: 528 Manor Street

Res: 528 Manor Street

Products: Beer, Ale

Facts: One of several bottlers at this address: John L. Coldren, H. C. Hallman, John Pontz, George Reese, J. Schwende, Nelson Springer, and Myers E. Wiley.

CONESTOGA BOTTLING WORKS
1917 - 1940 - BOTTLER

Bus: 113 Washington Street

Products: Soft Drink

Facts: Leon Cohn, manager.

COPLAND, JACOB
1879 - 1880 - BOTTLER

Bus: 125 -127 North Queen Street, 1879 - 1880

Res: 20 Dorwart Street, 1890 Laborer; moved to 730 Marietta Ave., 1897; Lab. & Res. West side of Fruitville Pike, north of the Pennsylvania Railroad

Facts: Owner of Copland Hotel, North Queen Street, 1888. Not listed in 1905 Directory.

CRYSTAL ROCK BEVERAGE COMPANY
1939 - 1942, 1953 - BOTTLER

Bus: 628 East Mifflin Street, 1939 - 1942; 817 North Cherry Street, 1953

Products: Mission, 7 Up and Tru Aid carbonated beverages

Facts: William F. Kleine, David Wentling, Earl J. Dempsey, managers

DIEHL, F. C. (FRANK)
1923 - 1924 - BOTTLER

Bus: 21 West Farnum Street, same address as P. P. Diehl (Father)

Facts: Listed as a student in 1923. Father tried to get him into business but it failed. Listed as clerk in 1931. No listing ever as a bottler; very scarce bottle.

DIEHL, P. P.
1923 - 1924 - BOTTLER

Bus: 125 Beaver Street, 21 West German Street (Now Farnum Street)

Facts: Worked for many years as the "master brewer" of Engle Bottling Works. Proprietor of Hotel Victoria, 452 High Street, 1899 - 1900. Proprietor of Fred Engle Bottling Works. That is the significance of the letter 'D' on Engle bottles, 1917 - 1928.

Biographies - Continued

DR. PEPPER BOTTLING COMPANY
BOTTLERS - DISTRIBUTORS

Bus: 132 - 134 East Madison Street

Products: Dr Pepper, Chuk-ker Beverages of Lancaster, Lancaster Club, Suncrest

DUKE, ROY E.
1940 - 1942 - BOTTLER

Bus: 127 - 143 Beaver Street, 1940; 423 South Queen Street

Facts: Facts per interview with Roy E. Duke, Jr., son of Roy E. Duke Sr., interview in 1990

Born in 1883. First worked as a carpenter. Rented the Engle Bottling Works, 1932. In 1940 became Beaver Bottling Works which lasted less than one year (reason Beaver bottle so scarce). Moved to 423 South Queen Street. Made soda from 1940 to 1942. In 1943 became Duke Distributors. Tore down old building in 1982. Forced out of business by larger competitors in 1990. Duke Distributors was Lancaster's largest Stroh's supplier.

EAGLE BOTTLING WORKS
1923 - 1924 - BOTTLER

Bus: 21 West Farnum Street. Same Location as P. P. Diehl.

Facts: Owned and operated by P. P. Diehl

EAST END BOTTLING WORKS
1889 - BOTTLER

Facts: No information on this bottle available.

EMPIRE BOTTLING WORKS
1868 - 1886 - BOTTLER

Bus: Lime and Locust streets; 143 East King Street

Facts: Lawrence Knapp was born in 1827 and came to America in 1847. He worked in breweries in Phila. until 1853. He worked with J. A. Sprenger in a three year partnership. Created a saloon and brewery at 135 Locust Street. Proprietor of Empire Steam Brewery. In 1886 Lawrence Knapp sold the brewery to Joseph Haefner. He fell through the floor of his barn and died of a ruptured kidney in 1894.

EMPIRE BOTTLING WORKS - JOSEPH HAEFNER
BREWER - BOTTLER

Bus: Lime and Locust Streets; 143 East King Street

Facts: Please see Haefner Brewery in the "History of the Breweries" section earlier in this book. There are very few bottles with both of these names as they were all transition bottles.

ENGEL BOTTLING WORKS, FRED
1912 - 1916 - BOTTLER

Facts: Misspelled variant, Engel should be Engle. Please see Engle Bottling Works, Fred below.

ENGLE, F. (FRED)
1871 - 1911 - BOTTLER

Bus.: 143 Beaver Street

Facts: Facts per interview with Godfrey Engle 2007.

The Fred Engle Bottling Company was in business for many years. Engle was born July 11, 1835. He was an active participant in the Civil War. At that time, his last name was listed as Engel, and he retained this spelling for several years; hence some of his bottles retain the Engel spelling. Upon returning from the war in 1871, he purchased John Casper's bottling business. He changed his name back to Engle shortly thereafter. Although he built and owned several homes in Lancaster, his business was located at 123 Beaver Street for many years. When Mr. Engle died on December 19, 1899, the business was

Biographies - Continued

purchased by P.P. Diehl and Roy E. Duke Sr. These gentlemen ran the business until 1928. The Engle bottles are, for the most part, very common with only a few scarce varieties. The authors have cataloged 35 different examples and undoubtedly there are more.

ENGLE BOTTLING WORKS, FRED
1912 - 1916 - BOTTLER

Bus: 123 Beaver Street

Facts: Different era within the same business as above. New management and marketing style, with definite change in bottle design and markings.

ENGLE BOTTLING WORKS 'D'
1917 - 1928 - BOTTLER

Bus: 123 Beaver Street

Facts: Different era within the same business as above. Now the business was owned and operated by P.P. Diehl, Roy E. Duke and James Buckius. You will notice that all of the bottles during this period of the Engle operations have a definitive 'D' on them. This is a reference to P. P. Diehl.

ENTERPRISE BOTTLING WORKS
1901 - 1904 - BOTTLER

Bus: 111- 113 Washington Street; 131- 133 South Water Street, 1903 - 1904. Address is same as Conestoga Bottling Works, perhaps a connection.

Products: Soft Drinks, Seltzers

Facts: Samuel Gerson, proprietor

FREY, W. B.
1899 - 1900 - BOTTLER

Bus: 434 West Walnut Street

Res: 811 Columbia Ave., 1894; 326 South Prince Street, 1897; 434 West Walnut Street, 1899 - 1900

Facts: Listed as a laborer in 1901

FULMER, A. P.
1882 - 1883 - BOTTLER

Bus: 14 Penn Square - restaurant and saloon

Res: 202 South Lime Street

Facts: Very rare label bottle; ran hotel in Rohrerstown, 1892; ran National Hotel, 1886

GERSTLY, W. F.
1899 - 1900 - BOTTLER

Bus: 522 East King Street

Facts: 1903 - 1912 listed at 522 East King Street as wine and liquor dealer. It appears that bottle with Gerstly name is not in above time period.

GIBSON, L. L.
1891 - BOTTLER

Bus: 120 North Charlotte Street

Res: 120 North Charlotte Street

Facts: Cabinet maker, 1890; bottler, 1891; wood finisher, 1892

G/R (GEORGE E. REESE)
1903 - 1910, 1913 - BOTTLER

Facts: Please see George E. Reese below.

GRIMECY, H. W. (HARRY)
1905 - 1920 - BOTTLER

Bus: 334 - 336 North Street

Res: 439 South Duke Street; 338 Concord Street, 1923

Facts: Listed as huckster, 1899; city sewer inspector, 1924; bottled for a number of years.

HLF & CO. (HENRY L. FRANKE)
1857 - 1860 - BREWER - BOTTLER

Bus: Prince & Walnut streets; 214 - 230 North Lime Street, 1874 1882

Biographies - Continued

Facts: Henry L. Franke was born in 1814 in the small town of Ludwigsburg, Baden, Germany. At the age of 30, he decided to come to the United States. As most of the early brewers, Henry came to Lancaster and started brewing lager beer. His first brewery and saloon were located at Prince and Walnut streets. In 1874, he decided to erect a much larger brewery and spent $50,000 at his new location at 216 North Lime Street. In 1872, he enlarged his old Prince Street establishment and it became the Franke Hotel. He later added a large hall at the rear and then changed the name to the Maennerchor Hotel. Henry Franke died on November 2, 1877.

HAEFNER BREWING COMPANY
1886 - 1945 - BREWER - BOTTLER

Bus: Lime and Locust streets, 143 East King Street

Facts: Please see detailed description of this brewer and bottler in the "History of the Breweries" section earlier in this book.

HAIN, CHARLES
1888 - 1894 - BOTTLER

Bus: Dorwart Street - 1888; 514 First Street, 1890 - 1894

Products: beer, porter, mineral water, fruit necture, aromatic ginger ale.

Facts: Proprietor of Southern Market Hotel, 49 S. Queen Street, 1899 - 1900

HALLMAN, H. C. (HARRY)
1897 - BOTTLER

Bus: 528 Manor Street

Res: 142-144 East King Street, 1897; 524 Manor Street, 1901; 14 South Queen Street; 139 East Chestnut, 1905 - 1906; 352 East New Street, 1909 - 1910

Facts: Bartender Leopard Hotel,1894-95; Bartender, 1903; Restaurant, 1905-06, 16 Penn Square. One of several bottlers at this address: John L. Coldren, H. C. Hallman, John Pontz, George Reese, J. Schwende, Nelson Springer, Myers E. Wiley.

HAMBRIGHT, W. A. (WILLIAM)
1890 - 1895 - BOTTLER

Bus: East Side of Ranck Ave., 2 blocks north of Philadelphia Pike

Res: 204 South Queen Street, 1873 -74; 602 West King Street, 1886; 9 West Orange Street, 1890

Facts: 1873-74 Rail Roader, not listed in directory after 1901

HANBRIGHT, W. A. (WILLIAM)
1890 - 1895 - BOTTLER

Facts: Misspelled bottle, should be Hambright, please see W. A. Hambright above.

HAUS, B. F.
1857 - BOTTLER

Bus.: East King between Duke and Lime streets

Res.: West King and South Water streets, 1859

Facts: Proprietor of Northern Market Hotel at 324 - 330 North Queen Street. Proprietor of Tremont Hotel, 165 North Queen Street

HYGRADE BOTTLING WORKS
1913 - 1928 - BOTTLER

Bus: 511 South Shippen Street, 1913-1916; Rear of 524 East King Street, 1917 - 1928

Facts: Harry W. Yonkers, owner - 1913 - 1915, Albert Harnish, manager - 1923 - 1928

Biographies - Continued

INGLESIDE BOTTLING WORKS
1897 - BOTTLER

Bus: Located south of Lancaster City, along South Prince Street

Facts: J. Zook, president, John J. Cochran, secretary, treasurer

J/S
1898 - 1901 AND 1916 - 1920 - BOTTLER

Facts: Please see J. Schwende below.

KEEFER, W.W.
1911 - 1918 - BOTTLER

Bus: 317 North Queen Street

Res: 408 North Queen Street - 1908

Products: Soda, sarsaparilla, birch beer, cream soda, ginger, cola, orange, Pottsville, Columbian, Rieker, Wacker, Haefner, Porter, ale, wines, liquor, sherry, root beer, cherry

Facts: Wine and liquor dealer, 1916 - 1918, son-in-law of George A. Kiehl

KEGEL, H. J.
1892 - BOTTLER

Bus: 434 East Orange Street

Res: 526 First Street, 1903; 218 West Walnut, 1911-12

Facts: Proprietor of Excelsior Hotel - 127 East King Street, 1892-95; proprietor of East End Hotel, 434 East Orange Street, 1892; proprietor of Bridgeport Hotel - south side of Philadelphia Pike, east of Conestoga Creek, 1899 - 1900; bartender - 1911 - 1912

KIEHL, GEORGE A.
1857 - 1891 - BOTTLER

Bus: 70 Chestnut Street, 1857; 75 East King Street, 1866 -1870; 168 East King Street

Res: 746 East King Street, 1873-1880

Products: Beer, mineral water, soda water

KIEHL & KEEFER
1898 - 1911 - BOTTLER

Bus: 70 Chestnut Street, 1857; 67- 75 East King Street, 1866; 168 East King Street

Res: 408 - 412 North Queen Street

Products: Wine and liquor dealer, also whiskey flasks are embossed with their names.

KIEHL & KEEFER - SCHLITZ
1898 - 1911 - BOTTLER

Products: Please see Kiehl & Keefer; this is only a variant. Schlitz on very bottom of bottle.

KIEHL & WACKER
1854 - 1865 - BOTTLER

Bus: Rear of 70 East Chestnut Street, 1857; Rear of 77 East King Street, 1859 - 1860

Res: George A. Kiehl - 746 East King Street, 1873 - 1880; Lime and Chestnut Streets

Products: Soda and mineral water

Facts: Kiehl's first venture that eventually became the Joseph Wacker brewery. George A. Kiehl and Kiehl's son-in-law, W.W. Keefer, eventually became Kiehl & Keefer.

KIST BOTTLING COMPANY
1950 - 1951 - BOTTLER

Bus: 239 North Water Street

Products: Soft drinks

KLUGH, ADAM M.
1895 - BOTTLER

Bus: 418 North Queen Street

Res: 418 North Queen Street

Biographies - Continued

Facts: 1895 bottler; 1899 umbrella maker; 1901-06 watch factory; 1907-08 lumber sales; 1911-12 salesman for J. Rohrer liquors; 1914 salesman for J. Wayne Hollinger liquor's store; 1925-28 piano store manager; 1929-30 life insurance salesman.

KRIMMEL, AUGUST
1894 - 1899 - BOTTLER

Bus: 515 Rockland Street at Green Street intersection, 1894

Res: 417 St. Joseph Street, 1886; 539 St. Joseph Street, 1899 -1900, office of coal company

Facts: 1886 - brick layer; 1904 - sold coal - 516 North Mulberry Street; 1917 - 1918, building contractor

LANCASTER BOTTLING COMPANY
C. G. BATES & SON, MGRS.
1899 - 1903 - BOTTLER

Bus: 234 West Lemon Street

Res: Roomed at 360 North Queen Street in 1899 - 1900

Facts: 1903 manager of Lancaster Bottling Company during this early period of the Company.

LANCASTER BOTTLING COMPANY
1937 - 1951 - BOTTLER

Bus: 620 East Mifflin Street, 1937 - 1943; 339 Beaver Street; 1944 - 1951

Products: Carbonated beverages, Golden Arrow, Red Rock, Conestoga Brand, ginger ale, imitation cherry soda

Facts: Please also see Lancaster Bottling Company - C. G. Bates for the early running of this company.

LANCASTER BOTTLING WORKS
1911 - 1912 - BOTTLER

Bus: 208 West Grant Street

Facts: Charles I. Wirth, proprietor.

LANCASTER BREWING INC. (OLD)
1946 - 1949 - BOTTLER

Little is known about this business

LANCASTER BREWING COMPANY (MODERN)
2003 - PRESENT - BREWER - BOTTLER

Bus: 302 N. Plum Street

Products.: Sells 7 brands of beer

Facts: This outstanding company replaced the Lancaster Malt Brewing Company in 2002. John Frantz owns the brewery which is now known for its unique brands.

LANCASTER MALT BREWING
1995 - 2002 - BREWER - BOTTLER

Bus: 302 N. Plum Street

Products: Sold 11 brands

Facts: Micheal Orlein, owner; sold to Lancaster Brewing Company in 2002.

MCGRANN, MICHAEL (MICHL)
1857 - 1864 - BOTTLER

Bus: 67 North Queen Street

Products: Porter, ale, cider

Facts: Proprietor of the White Horse Inn, east side of North Queen Street near the railroad. Some time before 1850, he moved his "White Horse" sign across the street to 148 North Queen Street. He also operated the Fairmont Inn at the corner of East King and Plum streets, until 1888.

Biographies - Continued

METROPOLITAN BOTTLING WORKS
1911 - 1912 - BOTTLER

Bus: 249 North Queen Street

Products: Also a distiller of wines and liquors

Facts: In 1919, the same address became Moses W. Katz Liquor Store; Lewis S. Cohen, bottler

METZGER BROS.
1897 - BOTTLER

Bus: 18 West King Street; 132 S. Christian Street

Facts: John, Charles F., and Harry F. are the brothers. They ran a hotel on the east end of King Street in the building that eventually became the Carl Fuss Heating and Cooling Co.

MIL-CO
BOTTLER

Facts: No information available for this bottler.

MILLER, PHILIP H.
1907 - 1911 - BOTTLER

Bus: 241 West Strawberry Street, same address as H. W. Ulmer, 1911 - 1918

Res: 241 West Strawberry Street, 1907-1911; 642 Hebrank Street, 1913; 478 Dorwart Street, 1916-1917

NEHI BOTTLING COMPANY
1931 - 1934 - BOTTLER

Bus: 200 Hazel Street

Res: W. L. Plitt, president

NORBECK, GEO S.
1899 - 1904 - BOTTLER

Bus: 208 West Grant Street

Res: 207 West King Street; 330 West King Street

Products: Beer, porter, ale, and also wholesale wines and liquors

Facts: Carriage maker, 1894 -1895, 128 - 144 East King Street; agent for Mountville Brick Company, 1911 - 1917, 20 North Queen Street; manager of Stevens House Cafe, 1903 - 1904

OLDE LANCASTER BREWING CO.
1938 - 1941 - BOTTLER

Bus: 201 West Walnut Street, same address as Wacker Bros.

Facts: The successors of Wacker Bros. Company.

PENN STAR BREWERY
1935 - 1938 - BOTTLER

Bus: 554 West King Street; office, 602 - 606 West King Street, Production Facility

Facts: Formerly Rieker Star Brewery, same building as Penn State Brewery

PENN STATE BREWERY
1931 - 1935 - BOTTLER

Bus: 554 West King Street; Office, 602 - 606 West King Street, Production Facility

Facts: Formerly Rieker Star Brewery, same building as Penn Star Brewery

PONTZ, JOHN (JNO)
1898 - 1900 - BOTTLER

Bus: 524 - 528 Manor Street

Biographies - Continued

Bus: 524 - 528 Manor Street

Res: 524 - 528 Manor Street

Facts: Proprietor of saloon, 123 Dorwart Street, 1882 - 1883; proprietor of the White Horse Hotel, 657 Manor Street, 1892; proprietor of Exchange Hotel, Mount Joy, East Main Street, 1892. One of several bottlers at this address: John L. Coldren, H. C. Hallman, George Reese, J. Schwende, Nelson Springer, Myers E. Wiley.

PURE BEVERAGE COMPANY
1923 - 1931 - BOTTLER

Bus: 138 North Mary Street, 1923 - 1924

Facts: Horace E. Heisey, proprietor; D. C. Brown, president and manager

QUADE, F. (FREDERICK)
1884 - 1888 - BOTTLER

Bus: 210 1/2 - 212 West King Street

Res: 212 West King Street, 1884 - 1886; West Strawberry near Water Street, 1868 - 1869

Facts: Butcher, 1884 - 1886; laborer, 1868 - 1869

REESE, GEORGE E.
1903 - 1910, 1913 - BOTTLER

Bus: 528 Manor Street

Res: 524 Manor Street

Facts: Ended bottling business in 1910 and then reopened for one year selling wines and liquors in 1913. Same address as Laura Wiley, wife of Myers E. Wiley, bottler. One of several bottlers at this address: John L. Coldren, H. C. Hallman, John Pontz, J. Schwende, Nelson Springer, Myers E. Wiley

RIEKER, FRANK A.
1882 - 1917 - BREWER - BOTTLER

Bus: 554 West King Street, office; 602 - 606 West King Street, production facility

Res: Corner of Marietta Ave. and Race Ave., built for for $12,995.

Facts: Please see detailed description of this brewer and bottler in the "History of the Breweries" section earlier in this book.

RUTTGERS WEISS BIER, C. (CONSTANTINE)
1887 - 1888 - BOTTLER

Bus: 26 E. Frederick Street

Res: 607 St. Joseph Street, 1875 - 1876

Products: Lager beer and ale

Facts: Physician, 1875 - 1876

SHAEFFER, A. B. (ALFRED)
1879 - 1891 - BOTTLER

Bus: 13 East Orange Street

Res: Grofftown Road between Orange and East Chestnut streets, 1888; room at 133 West King Street, 1903 - 1904

Facts: Beer, wines and liquors; proprietor of Grofftown Distillery, 951 East Orange Street, 1901.

SCHMIDT, J. & CO.
1899 - 1902 - BOTTLER

Bus: 239 West Strawberry Street

Res: 554 South Lime Street

Facts: Same address as J. Schwende

SCHMITT & BEILMAN
1890 - 1906 - BOTTLER

Bus: 239 Strawberry Street

Res: 241 Strawberry Street, 1890 - 1906; lab at 142 Love Ave., southeast of Manor St. to Seymour St. - Schmitt; 421 Fremont Street -

Biographies - Continued

Beilman, 302 West Church Street; 1908 - 1910 - Schmitt, 233 Church Street; 1911 - 1918 - Beilman

Facts: Florenz Schmitt - William Beilman. Schmitt, laborer, 142 Love Ave. southeast from Manor St. to Seymour St.; grocer, 1908 - 1910; also a night watchman

SCHWENDE, J.
1898 - 1901 AND 1916 -1920 - BOTTLER

Bus: 239 West Strawberry Street, 1898; 528 Manor Street, 1916 - 1920

Res: 536 West Vine Street, same address as J. Schmitt, 1898; 528 Manor Street, 1916 - 1917; 614 East King Street; 1919 - 1920

Facts: Proprietor of Hotel Victoria, 450 High St., 1901; proprietor of Swan Hotel, 1903 - 1904. One of several bottlers at this address: John L. Coldren, H. C. Hallman, John Pontz, George Reese, Nelson Springer, Myers E. Wiley

SEVEN UP BOTTLING COMPANY
1962 - 1964 - BOTTLER

Bus: 759 Flory Mill Road

SHADEL (CHARLES)
1899 - 1902 - BOTTLER

Bus: 514 First Street

Res: 514 First Street

Facts: Proprietor of the Fountain Inn, 32 - 34 South Queen Street, 1892 - 1895.

SPRENGER BOTTLER
1896 - 1951 - BOTTLER - BREWER

Facts: Please see Sprenger Brewing Company

SPRENGER BREWING COMPANY
1896 - 1951 - BOTTLER - BREWER

Bus: South Lime and Locust streets

Products: Pilsner, bock, cream ale, porter, Old Münchner, lager, Old English

Facts: Please see detailed description of this brewer and bottler in the "History of the Breweries" section earlier in this book.

SPRENGER COMPANY, THE
1896 - 1951 - BOTTLER - BREWER

Facts: Please see Sprenger Brewing Company

SPRENGER, E. E. (ELIZABETH)
1888 - 1908 - BOTTLER

Bus: 31 South Lime Street

Res: 4 West Walnut Street

Facts: Widow of George F. Sprenger, ran business after George's death. Also same address as John F. Bair and Bair & Groff.

SPRENGER, G. F. (GEORGE)
1877 - 1888 - BOTTLER

Bus: 31 South Lime Street

Res: 4 West Walnut Street

Products: Malt liquors, cream ales, mineral water, and various types of lager and imported beer

Facts: The famous Sprenger family had a younger brother of J.A. and J.J. Sprenger. He was George F. and was born in 1842, more than a decade after his older brothers. George F. operated a bottling works at 31 South Lime Street for several years. Little else is known about this younger Sprenger brother. His obituary states he died in 1888. Wife was E.E. Sprenger.

SPRENGER, J. A.
1859 - 1884 - BOTTLER - BREWER

Bus: 54 East King Street, saloon and brewery, 1866 - 1872; 125 - 131 East King Street, 1873 - 1880; 16 North Prince Street, 1882 - 1883; 209 - 211 Locust Street, 1886

Res: 18 North Prince - 1886

Biographies - Continued

Facts: Please see detailed description of this brewer and bottler in the "History of the Breweries" section earlier in this book.

SPRENGER, J. J.
1857 - 1874 - BOTTLER - BREWER

Bus: Walnut and Water streets, 1857; 129 East King Street, 1873 - 1874

Res: 70 East Chestnut Street, 1857; 150 East Chestnut Street, 1873 - 1874

Facts: Please see detailed description of this brewer and bottler in the "History of the Breweries" section earlier in this book.

SPRENGER, J. J. & J. A.
1857 - 1859 - BOTTLER - BREWER

Bus: 125 - 131 East King Street

Facts: Please see detailed description of this brewer and bottler in the "History of the Breweries" section earlier in this book.

SPRINGER, E. E. (ELIZABETH)
1892 - BOTTLER

Facts: Misspelled Springer should be Sprenger, please see E. E. Sprenger above.

SPRINGER, NELSON H.
1932 - BOTTLER

Bus: 528 Manor Street

Res: 124 S. Prince Street, 1931; 217 East King Street, 1939 - 1940

Facts: Worked for Central Cooperative Company, 1931; March 19, 1932, federal agents found 128 barrels of beer on his property at the rear of the 500 block of Manor Street off Lafayette Street; 1939 - 1940, mechanic. One of several bottlers at this address: John L. Coldren, H. C. Hallman, John Pontz, George Reese, J. Schwende, Myers E. Wiley.

STAR BOTTLING COMPANY
1889 BOTTLER

Bus: 1 West Orange Street

STAR BOTTLING WORKS
1909 - 1928 BOTTLER

Bus: 445 South Christian Street, 1909 - 1916; 534 Chester Street, 1917 - 1928

Facts: High grade beverages, Hires root beer, Hires ginger ale, orange soda, cherry soda, raspberry soda, cream soda, sarsaparilla, lime and lemon soda, and birch beer

STAR BREWING & BOTTLING COMPANY
1890 BOTTLER

Bus: 1 West Orange Street

Facts: This is the only Lancaster bottle with a Jewish "Star of David". William A. Hambright, manager.

SUNCREST BOTTLING COMPANY

Please see Dr. Pepper Bottling Company

TODD, HARRY
1903 - 1906 - BOTTLER

Bus: 207 West King Street, 1903 - 1904; 208 Grant Street, 1905 - 1906

Res: 434 Poplar Street, 1901 - 1904 and 1907 - 1908

Facts: Bartender, 1901 - 1904; proprietor of Lafayette Hotel, 527 North Christian Street, 1907 - 1912; proprietor of Southern Market Hotel, South Queen and Vine streets, 1913 - 1917; also a wine and liquor dealer.

TRETTER, JOHN N.
1899 - 1918 - BOTTLER

Bus: 336 North Street

Res: 327 Locust Street

Biographies - Continued

TRETTER, JOHN N. & SON
1905 - 1914 - BOTTLER

Bus: 336 North Street

Res: 327 Locust Street

ULMER, H. W. (HIRAM)
1903 - 1906 - BOTTLER

Bus: 241 West Strawberry Street; same address as Philip Miller.

Res: 531 Chester Street, 1903 - 1904; 405 Howard Ave., 1923 - 1924

Facts: Cook, 1903 - 1904; proprietor of Western Hotel, 202 West Orange Street, 1911 - 1914

WACKER BREWING CO. (OLD)
1870 -1880 - BOTTLER-BREWER

Bus: 223 West Walnut Street

Facts: Please see detailed description of this brewer and bottler in the "History of the Breweries" section earlier in this book.

WACKER BREWING CO. (NEW)
1938-1956 - BOTTLER-BREWER

Bus: 223 West Walnut Street

Facts: Please see detailed description of this brewer and bottler in the "History of the Breweries" section earlier in this book.

WACKER BROTHERS
1880-1938 - BOTTLER-BREWER

Bus: 223 West Walnut Street

Facts: Please see detailed description of this brewer and bottler in the "History of the Breweries" section earlier in this book.

WACKER, JOSEPH
1870-1880 - BOTTLER-BREWER

Bus: 223 West Walnut Street

Facts: Please see detailed description of this brewer and bottler in the "History of the Breweries" section earlier in this book.

WALKER, THOMAS
1882-1883 - BOTTLER

Bus: 311 Middle Ave. (now Howard Ave.)

WALL, GEORGE
1886 -1887 - BOTTLER

Bus: 406 South Queen Street

Res: 321 South Queen Street

Facts: Owner of grocery store, 401 High Street, 1873 - 1874; owner of Southern Exchange Hotel, corner of South Queen St. and Middle Ave (now Howard Ave), 1874 - 1892; 1884, sold groceries and feed at corner of High and Strawberry streets, proprietor of Wall House, 321 - 325 South Queen Street.

WANBAUGH & HAINES
1890 - BOTTLERS

Bus: Unknown

Res: 425 North Cherry Street - Wanbaugh
35 North Shippen Street - Haines

Facts: Israel H. Wanbaugh, carpenter
Joel L. Haines, auctioneer, real estate

WARE, E. C. (EPHRAIM)
1850 - 1853 - BOTTLER

Bus: 209 Lime Street

Res: 209 Lime Street

Facts: Born in New Jersey in 1817, listed in the 1850 census at 209 Lime Street. Started bottling business in Philadelphia in 1846, and moved to Lancaster in 1850. Ran bottling business in Lancaster until 1853. He then moved back to Philadelphia and continued bottling until 1857. That is the reason there are both Philadelphia and Lancaster variants of this bottle, and the reference to Union Glass Works, Philadelphia on one of the Lancaster variants. **Thanks to the Philadelphia Bottle Book Group, and Tod von Mechow for this information.**

Biographies - Continued

WEBER, GEORGE
1890 - 1892 - BOTTLER

Bus: 515 Rockland Street

Res: 515 Rockland Street

Facts: Hotel, 353 West King Street

WHISTLE BOTTLING COMPANY
1920 - 1931 - BOTTLER

Bus: 317 North Queen Street, 1920 - 1924; 22 West Clay Street, 1925 - 1931

Products: Malt & hops, cereal beverages, soft drinks, fruit beverages

Facts: W. W. Keefer, proprietor, 1923 - 1931

WILEY, MYERS E.
1909 -1912 - BOTTLER

Bus: 528 Manor Street, 1909 - 1912

Res: Laborer, north side of Harrisburg Pike, west of College Ave., 1907 - 1908; 524 Manor Street, 1909 - 1912

Facts: One of several bottlers at this address: John L. Coldren, H. C. Hallman, John Pontz, George Reese, J. Schwende, Nelson Springer.

WOLPERT, PETER K.
1890 -1892 - BOTTLER

Bus: 407 - 409 West King Street

Res: 549 Saint Joseph Street, 1884; 614 First Street, 1890 - 1892, 516 First Street, 1892 - 1896

Facts: Proprietor, Green Tree Hotel, 407 - 409 West King Street, 1899 - 1900; proprietor, Western Market Hotel, 602 - 604 West King Street. This was Frank A. Rieker's bar room at the brewery. He was also a debt collector for Frank A. Rieker.

ZECH, CHARLES (CHAS)
1886 -1920 - BOTTLER

Bus: 691 - 705 West Orange Street (West Orange Street and Columbia Ave)

Res: 707 West Orange Street

Facts: Brewery for four years.

Charles Zech was born in Wurttemberg, Germany on May 18, 1851. It is reported that he came to America in 1869. He moved to Lancaster from Reading in June of 1876, and took a job as a foreman at Franke's Brewery for a short time. He then went to Frank A. Rieker's brewery where he was again hired as a foreman. In 1886, he went into business for himself, and ran his bottling business for many years. His bottling works and brewery was located along the West Orange Street and Columbia Ave. intersection. For a short period, from 1894 to 1897, he brewed and bottled beer at this location. At the same location and later at 14 North Charlotte Street, the company bottled soft drinks of many different types until the early 1960's. Charles Zech was married to Rosa Spangler and they had five children. He died on April 11, 1937. The Columbia Ave. location later became the Robert Hall Clothing Store for many years, and then was occupied by a beauty supply company. It is a real challenge for collectors who strive to obtain every variety of Zech bottles. As you can see, there are over 35 different variants listed. There are probably a few that the authors have missed.

ZECK, CHARLES (CHAS)
1886 -1920 - BOTTLER

Facts: Misspelled variant, please see Charles Zech above.

INSTRUCTIONS FOR USING THIS GUIDE
RARITY SCALE

Each bottle listed has been given a rarity rating of R-1, R-2, etc. The method is a very simple one and each "R" number represents a specific estimate on observations and records covering many years.

- R-1   Common
- R-2   Scarce
- R-3   Very Scarce
- R-4   Rare
- R-5   Very Rare
- R-6   Extremely Rare
- R-7   Unique – One of a Kind

The rarity of bottles has been determined and based upon the most recent and accurate information obtained from collectors and our research. The authors know that other items may exist that have not been included. We have created a submission form on www.lancasterbottlebooks.com to assist in documenting any items not listed in this book.

REGARDING VALUATIONS

In view of changing trends and available information, it seems unwise (if not impossible) to give values in a permanent type book such as this.

NUMBERING SYSTEM

The master numbers for each brewer or bottler begin with the number 101 for the first variety listed. Each subsequent variety follows in progression; i.e., 102, 103, 104, etc. This numbering system allows for the addition of any new variants that may be identified in the future.

LABEL VALUATIONS

In the latter years of bottling, embossing became less common as paper labels became more cost effective. In most cases, the value of a labeled bottle is not in the bottle but the condition of the label. Because labels are paper, it is very difficult to find them in mint condition. Many times the information on the label or the scarcity of the label creates its value. Occasionally, during the transition from embossing to labels, a few very rare labels were placed on embossed bottles.

INSTRUCTIONS FOR USING THIS GUIDE - Continued

    1   2   3   4

If you examine the labels above, you can see that the labels on bottles 1 and 2 are in near mint condition. Notice that the colors are bright and vibrant and that there are no tears, missing edges, or missing pieces of the label. You will also notice on bottles 3 and 4 that the colors are less vibrant. There are stains and missing edges and actual missing parts of the labels. In determining the value of a label in the examples above, if all four labels were of equal rarity, labels 1 and 2 would be far more valuable. In determining rarity of a label, most times it is the number of known examples of the label or the information on the label. Key indicators are the actual Lancaster, PA city name, the bottler or brewer name, Federal Tax ID's, contents, and if the label is Pre-Prohibition.

NOTE: Some collectors of Lancaster bottles and others have alerted us of new information and bottles of which we were not aware when we began the printing of volume one. As we continue the printing and numbering of the 500 limited edition copies of this guide we have included these discoveries.

The new items are identified by red lettering of the variant number and the description text.

For those that have previously purchased our guide, you may download these updates from our website at www.lancasterbottlebooks.com.

OVERVIEW OF EACH BOTTLE

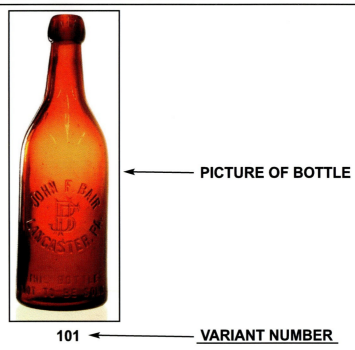

← PICTURE OF BOTTLE

101 **← VARIANT NUMBER**

Amber, 9.50", Top-Blob, Type-Blob, Bot-Smooth, R-4, Most difficult variant **← BOTTLE DETAIL**

COLORS

Clear	Med Green
Aqua	Dark Green
Amber	Olive Green
Honey Amber	Dark Olive Green
Dark Amber	Modern Green
Apple Green	Cobalt Blue
Light Green	

TYPE TOPS

Double-Taper Applied Top
Single-Taper Applied Top
Applied Top
Blob Top
Crown Top

TYPE BOTTOMS

Iron Pontil
Sand Pontil
Smooth Base

BOTTLE TYPES

Blob	Squat
Small Blob	Hutch
Small Crown	16 oz. Hutch
Crown	Quart Hutch
Gravitating Stopper	3-Piece Beer
Pony	Codds
Soft Drink	

Each bottle listed has been given a rarity rating of R-1, R-2, etc. The method is a very simple one and each "R" number represents a specific estimate on observations and records covering many years.

R-1	Common		R-5	Very Rare
R-2	Scarce		R-6	Extremely Rare
R-3	Very Scarce		R-7	Unique – One of a Kind
R-4	Rare			

RARITY SCALE ONLY APPLIES TO ITEMS IN CURRENT VOLUME

BAIR, JOHN F.

101

Amber, 9.50", Top-Blob, Type-Blob, Bot-Smooth, R-4, Most difficult variant

102

Clear, 6.50", Top-Bob, Type-Pony, Bot-Smooth, R-4

103

Clear, 7.50", Top-Blob, Type-Blob, Bot-Smooth, R-3, Very unusual size and height of bottle

104

Aqua, 7.0", Top-Blob, Type-Hutch, Bot-Smooth, R-3

105

Clear, 7.0", Top-Blob, Type-Hutch, Bot-Smooth, R-3

106

Apple Green, 6.25", Top-Blob, Type-Hutch, Bot-Smooth, R-3

BAIR, JOHN F. - Continued

107

Aqua, 6.25", Top-Blob,
Type-Hutch, Bot-Smooth,
R-3

108

Aqua, 9.50", Top-Blob,
Type-Blob, Bot-Smooth,
R-2

109

Clear, 9.50", Top-Blob,
Type-Blob, Bot-Smooth,
R-2

110

Clear, 9.25", Top-Crown,
Type-Crown, Bot-Smooth,
R-2

111

Clear, 9.50", Top-Blob,
Type-Blob, Bot-Smooth,
R-3

112

Clear, 9.50", Top-Blob,
Type-Blob, Bot-Smooth,
R-3

BAIR & GROFF

101

Aqua, 9.00", Top-Blob,
Type-Blob, Bot-Smooth,
R-4

102

Aqua, 6.50", Top-Bob,
Type-Hutch, Bot-Smooth,
R-4

BEAVER BOTTLING WORKS

101

Aqua, 7.50", Top-Crown, Type-Crown,
Bot-Smooth, R-6, similar slug plate to
Eagle Bottling Works, extremely rare

BERTL, LOUIS

101

Clear, 9.50", Top-Blob,
Type-Blob, Bot-Smooth,
R-4

102

Aqua, 9.50, Top-Blob,
Type-Blob, Bot-Smooth,
R-4

103

Aqua, 6.50, Top-Blob,
Type-Hutch, Bot-Smooth,
R-4

104

Aqua, 6.50, Top-Blob,
Type-Hutch, Bot-Smooth,
R-4

BRYDEN, A. M.

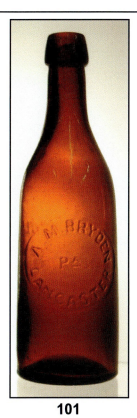
101
Dark Amber, 9.25", Top-Blob, Type-Blob, Bot-Smooth, R-5

102
Honey Amber, 9.25", Top-Bob, Type-Blob, Bot-Smooth, R-6, this color extremely rare

103
Aqua, 11.50", Top-Blob, Type-Blob, Bot-Smooth, R-5, rare quart size

C. G. & CO. (Charles Grove & Company)

101
Cobalt Blue, 7.25", Top-Applied Top, Type-Squat, Bot-Iron Pontil, R-7, unique

102
Dark Green, 7.25", Top-Applied Top, Type-Squat, Bot-Iron Pontil, R-5

CASPER, J. (John)

101

Blue Green, 6.75", Top-Double Taper, Type-Squat, Bot-Smooth, R-4

102

Apple Green, 6.50, Top-Double Taper, Type-Squat, Bot-Smooth, R-6, very rare color

103

Aqua, 6.75, Top-Double Taper, Type-Squat, Bot-Smooth, R-6, very rare color

104

Dark Green, 6.75, Top-Double Taper, Type-Squat, Bot-Smooth, R-5

105

Apple Green, 7.25", Top-Applied Top, Type-Squat, Bot-Smooth, R-6, very rare color

106

Aqua, 7.25, Top-Applied Top, Type-Squat, Bot-Smooth, R-2

CASPER, J. (John) - Continued | CASPER, J & H

107

108

101

Aqua, 7.25, Top-Applied Top, Type-Gravitating Stopper, Bot-Smooth, R-4, J. Casper not John Casper

Aqua, 7.25, Top-Applied Top, Type-Gravitating Stopper, Bot-Smooth, R-4, John Casper, first name spelled out

Med Green, 7.00", Top-Double Taper, Type-Squat, Bot-Smooth, R-4

CASPER, J & H - Continued

102

103-Front

103-Rear

Green, 7.50, Top-Applied Top, Type-Squat, Bot-Iron Pontil, R-3

Blue Green, 7.50, Top-Applied Top, Type-Squat, Bot-Iron Pontil, R-5

Blue Green, 7.50, Top-Applied Top, Type-Squat, Bot-Iron Pontil, R-5

CASPER, J & H - Continued

104-Front

Aqua, 7.50, Top-Applied Top, Type-Squat, Bot-Smooth, R-4

105-Front

Med Green, 7.50, Top-Applied Top, Type-Squat, Bot-Smooth, R-6

105-Rear

Med Green, 7.50, Top-Applied Top, Type-Squat, Bot-Smooth, R-6

106

Aqua, 6.00", Top-Applied Top, Type-Blob, Bot-Smooth, R-5, Cold Cream Soda, misspelled Caspar

107

Light Green, 6.50, Top-Double Taper, Type-Squat, Bot-Smooth, R-5

108

Dark Green, 7.00, Top-Double Taper, type-Squat, Bot-Smooth, R-6, misspelled J&N, should be J&H

CASPER, J & H - Continued

109
Aqua, 6.50, Top-Double Taper, Type-Squat, Bot-Smooth, R-6

110
Aqua, 6.50, Top-Applied Top, Type-Squat, Bot-Iron Pontil, R-6

111
Dark Green, 6.50, Top-Double Taper, Type-Squat, Bot-Smooth, R-6

CASPER, J & N

Please see J&H Casper above, misspelled J&N, should be J&H

CHAMBERLIN, W. C.

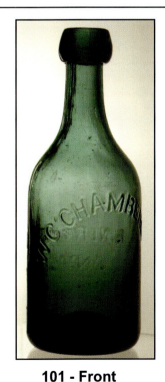
101 - Front
Dark Green, 7.50", Top-Applied Top, Type-Squat, Bot-Iron Pontil, R-4

101-102 -Rear
Dark Green, 7.50", Top-Applied Top, Type-Squat, Bot-Iron Pontil, R-4

102
Blue Green, 7.50", Top-Applied Top, Type-Squat, Bot-Iron Pontil, R-6

CHUK-KER BOTTLING WORKS

There is no information available to believe that there was ever a company called Chuk-ker Bottling Works, operating in Lancaster. The authors believe this bottle was really a Dr. Pepper bottle labeled Chuk-ker Bottling Works. The Chuk-ker name was marketed and sold nationwide under various distributors. See Dr. Pepper

COCA-COLA BOTTLING WORKS

101
Light Green, 7.75", Top-Crown, Type-Soft Drink, Bot-Smooth, R-1

102
Aqua, 7.75", Top-Crown, Type-Soft Drink, Bot-Smooth, R-1

103
Aqua, 7.75", Top-Crown, Type-Soft Drink, Bot-Smooth, R-1

104
Light Green, 7.75", Top-Crown, Type-Soft Drink, Bot-Smooth, R-2, Christmas soda date

105
Light Green, 7.75", Top-Crown, Type-Soft Drink, Bot-Smooth, R-1, Small Lancaster on bottom

106
Light Green, 7.75", Top-Crown, Type-Soft Drink, Bot-Smooth, R-1

COCA-COLA BOTTLING WORKS - Continued

107
Clear, 7.75", Top-Crown, Type-Soft Drink, Bot-Smooth, R-1, Soda Water, Coca Cola bottom front of bottle

108
Clear, 7.75", Top-Crown, Type-Soft Drink, Bot-Smooth, R-1, Soda Water, Coca Cola bottom front of bottle, also large Lancaster on bottom of bottle

109
Aqua, 6.0", Top-Crown, Type-Soft Drink, Bot-Smooth, R-1, Commemorative 2000 All American City Label

110
Clear, 7.75", Top-Crown, Type-Soft Drink, Bot-Smooth, R-1, Crass brand, pyro label red & white

111
Clear, 9.50", Top-Crown, Type-Soft Drink, Bot-Smooth, R-1, Crass brand, pyro label red & white

112
Clear, 7.75", Top-Crown, Type-Soft Drink, Bot-Smooth, R-1, Crass brand, pyro label green & yellow

COCA-COLA BOTTLING WORKS - Continued

113

Clear, 9.50", Top-Crown, Type-Soft Drink, Bot-Smooth, R-1, Crass brand, pyro label green & yellow

114

Clear, 9.50", Top-Crown, Type-Soft Drink, Bot-Smooth, R-1, Crass brand, pyro label green & yellow

115

Modern green, 7.75", Top-Crown, Type-Soft Drink, Bot-Smooth, R-3, Crass Pale Dry, Lancaster, PA on Bottom

COCA-COLA BOTTLING WORKS   COLDREN, JOHN

116

Clear, 7.75", Top-Crown, Type-Soft Drink, Bot-Smooth, R-1, Simillar to 107 & 108, Soda Water, Coca Cola Bott Co., bottom of bottle

101

Clear, 9.50", Top-Blob, Type-Blob, Bot-Smooth, R-5, 528 Manor Street on front of bottle

CONESTOGA BOTTLING WORKS

101

Aqua, 7.50", Top-Crown, Type-Soft Drink, Bot-Smooth, R-3, 113 Washington Street on front of bottle

102

Clear, 7.75", Top-Crown, Type-Soft Drink, Bot-Smooth, R-3

COPLAND, JACOB

101

Aqua, 9.25", Top-Blob, Type-Blob, Bot-Smooth, R-5, Smooth

CRYSTAL ROCK BEVERAGE COMPANY

101

Modern Green, 8.00", Top-Crown, Type-Soft Drink, Bot-Smooth, R-2, White pyro label

102-103-104-Front

Clear, 7.75", Top-Crown, Type-Soft Drink, Bot-Smooth, R-1, Black & White pyro label

102-Rear

Clear, 7.75", Top-Crown, Type-Soft Drink, Bot-Smooth, R-1

103-Rear

Clear, 7.75", Top-Crown, Type-Soft Drink, Bot-Smooth, R-1, larger label on rear, similar to variant 102

104-Rear

Clear, 7.75", Top-Crown, Type-Soft Drink, Bot-Smooth, R-3, label states Naturally Clear on rear of bottle

CRYSTAL ROCK BEVERAGE COMPANY - Continued

105

Modern Green, 8.00", Top-Crown, Type-Soft Drink, Bot-Smooth, R-2

106

Clear, 7.25", Top-Crown, Type-Soft Drink, Bot-Smooth, R-2

107

Clear, 9.25", Top-Crown, Type-Soft Drink, Bot-Smooth, R-2

DIEHL, F. C.

101

Aqua, 7.75", Top-Crown, Type-Crown, Bot-Smooth, R-4

DIEHL, P. P.

101

Aqua, 7.75", Top-Crown, Type-Crown, Bot-Smooth, R-3

DR. PEPPER BOTTLING WORKS

101 - 102 - Front

Clear, 8.00", Top-Crown, Type-Soft Drink, Bot-Smooth, R-2, Embossed 10 - 2 - 4 on front

101-Bottom

102-Bottom

103

Clear, 8.50", Top-Crown, Type-Soft Drink, Bot-Smooth, R-2, Lancaster Club brand, red and white pyro

104

Clear, 7.00", Top-Crown, Type-Soft Drink, Bot-Smooth, R-3, Lancaster Club brand, red and white pyro

105-106 Front

Clear, 7.50", Top-Crown, Type-Soft Drink, Bot-Smooth, R-2, Chuk-ker brand, red and white pyro, Dr. Pepper

106-Rear

Clear, 7.50", Top-Crown, Type-Soft Drink, Bot-Smooth, R-4, Chuk-ker brand, red and white pyro, states bottled by Chuk-ker Beverages, is a mislabel should be Dr. Pepper.

51

DR. PEPPER BOTTLING WORKS - Continued

107 - 108 - Front

Clear, 8.50", Top-Crown, Type-Soft Drink, Bot-Smooth, R-2, Suncrest brand, blue and white

108 - Rear

Clear, 8.50", Crown, Soft Drink, Smooth, R-2, Suncrest brand, blue and white pyro, bottle states bottled by SunCrest Bottling Company. Authors believe this is similar to the Chukker bottle, in that there is no evidence of a company called Suncrest Bottling Company operating in Lancaster, PA. The Sun Crest brand was marketed and distributed nationwide. This bottle is a misprint, should state Dr. Pepper.

DUKE, ROY E.

101

Aqua, 8.00", Top-Crown, Type-Crown, Bot-Smooth, R-2, Similar slug plate as F. C. and P. P. Diehl bottle

102

Clear, 8.00", Top-Crown, type-Crown, Bot-Smooth, R-2

DUKE, ROY E. - Continued

103

Aqua, 8.00", Top-Crown, type-Crown, Bot-Smooth, R-2

104

Clear, 8.50", Top-Crown, Type-Crown, Bot-Smooth, R-3, Howdy both ways on label

EAGLE BOTTLING WORKS

EAST END BOTTLING WORKS

101

Clear, 7.75", Top-Crown, Type-Crown, Bot-Smooth, R-6, extremely rare

102

Aqua, 7.75", Top-Crown, Type-Crown, Bot-Smooth, R-7

102 - Bottom

Chas. Zech bottle, states Property of Eagle Bottling Works, contents only sold, Bottle Loaned

101

Clear, 9.50", Top-Blob, Type-Blob, Bot-Smooth, R-5

53

EMPIRE BOTTLING WORKS

101

Aqua, 6.50", Top-Blob,
Type-Hutch, Bot-Smooth,
R-3

102

Aqua, 6.50", Top-Blob,
Type-Hutch, Bot-Smooth,
R-3

103

Clear, 9.50", Top-Blob,
Type-Blob, Bot-Smooth,
R-1

104

Clear, 9.25", Top-Blob,
Type-Blob, Bot-Smooth,
R-1

105

Clear, 9.50", Top-Blob,
Type-Blob, Bot-Smooth,
R-1

106

Amber, 9.50", Top-Blob,
Type-Blob, Bot-Smooth,
R-2

EMPIRE BOTTLING WORKS - Continued

107
Clear, 9.50", Top-Blob,
Type-Blob, Bot-Smooth,
R-1

108
Clear, 9.50", Top-Blob,
Type-Blob, Bot-Smooth,
R-1

109
Aqua, 9.25", Top-Blob, Type-Blob,
Bot-Smooth, R-3, This bottle is
Registered Not to be Sold on
bottom front of bottle

110
Honey Amber, 9.50", Top-
Blob, Type-Blob, Bot-
Smooth, R-4

EMPIRE BOTTLING WORKS - Continued

111

Clear, 9.50", Top-Crown,
Type-Crown, Bot-Smooth,
R-1

112

Amber, 9.50", Top-Crown,
Type-Crown, Bot-Smooth,
R-3

113

Amber, 9.25", Top-Blob,
Type-Blob, Bot-Smooth,
R-2

114

Aqua, 9.50", Top-Crown,
Type-Crown, Bot-Smooth,
R-1

EMPIRE BOTTLING WORKS - Continued

115
Clear, 9.50", Top-Crown, Type-Crown, Bot-Smooth, R-1

116
Clear, 9.25", Top-Crown, Type-Crown, Bot-Smooth, R-2

117
Clear, 9.25", Top-Crown, Type-Crown, Bot-Smooth, R-3, Large E

EMPIRE BOTTLING WORKS - Joseph Haefner

101-Front
Joseph Haefner Label, Empire Bottling Works. Was used as the transition bottle when he purchased the Empire Bottling Works, R-6

101-Rear
Label was placed on an Empire Bottling Works Variant No. 115

102
Aqua, 9.50", Top-crow, Type-Crown, Bot-Smooth, R-3, also transition bottle

ENGEL BOTTLING WORKS, THE FRED

Please see Engle Bottling Works, The Fred below, misspelled Engel, should be Engle

ENGLE, F. (Fred)

101

Blue Green, 6.75", Top-Double Taper, Type-Squat, Bot-Smooth, R-5

102

Aqua, 7.00", Top-Double Taper, Type-Squat, Bot-Smooth, R-4

103

Aqua, 7.00", Top-Applied Top, Type-Squat, Bot-Smooth, R-1

104

Aqua, 6.75", Top-Blob, Type-Hutch, Bot-Smooth, R-2, Panel Base

105

Aqua, 6.75", Top-Blob, Type-Hutch, Bot-Smooth, R-2, Panel Base

106

Aqua, 7.25", Top-Blob, Type Gravitating Stopper, Bot-Smooth, R-5, Small Slug

ENGLE, F. (Fred) - Continued

107

Aqua, 7.00", Top-Blob, Type Gravitating Stopper, Bot-Smooth, R-4

108

Aqua, 9.25, Top-Blob, Type-Blob, Bot-Smooth, R-1

109

Aqua, 9.50, Top-Blob, Type-Blob, Bot-Smooth, R-1

110

Aqua, 9.50, Top-Blob, Type-Blob, Bot-Smooth, R-1

111

Aqua, 9.00, Top-Blob, Type-Blob, Bot-Smooth, R-1

112

Aqua, 9.25, Top-Blob, Type-Blob, Bot-Smooth, R-1

ENGLE, F. (Fred) - Continued

113

Aqua, 9.50, Top-Blob, Type-Blob, Bot-Smooth, R-1

114

Aqua, 9.00, Top-Blob, Type-Blob, Bot-Smooth, R-1

115

Aqua, 9.25, Top-Blob, Type-Blob, Bot-Smooth, R-3

116

Aqua, 9.00, Top-Blob, Type-Blob, Bot-Smooth, R-3

117

Green, 11.25, Top-Blob, Type-Soft Drink, Bot-Smooth, R-7

118

Clear, 6.75", Top-Blob, Type-Hutch, Bot-Smooth, R-4, Panel Base

ENGLE BOTTLING WORKS, THE FRED

101

Aqua, 7.00", Top-Blob, Type-Hutch, Bot-Smooth, R-4, Panel Base

102

Clear, 9.25", Top-Blob, Type-Blob, Bot-Smooth, R-2

103

Clear, 9.25", Top-Blob, Type-Blob, Bot-Smooth, R-2, Lady Leg Neck

104-Rear

104

Clear, 9.75", Top-Blob, Type-Blob, Bot-Smooth, R-4, monogram on rear, Panel base

105

Amber, 9.50", Top-Blob, Type-Blob, Bot-Smooth, R-3, Engle misspelled Engel, Panel Base

106

Aqua, 9.50", Top-Blob, Type-Blob, Bot-Smooth, R-3, Engle misspelled Engel, Panel Base

ENGLE BOTTLING WORKS 'D'

101

Clear, 7.50", Top-Blob, Type-Pony, Bot-Smooth, R-3

102

Aqua, 7.75", Top-Blob, Type-Pony, Bot-Smooth, R-3, states registered 1889 on bottom rear

103

Clear, 9.75", Top-Blob, Type-Blob, Bot-Smooth, R-2

104

Clear, 9.50", Top-Blob, Type-Blob, Bot-Smooth, R-2

105

Clear, 9.00", Top-Blob, Type-Blob, Bot-Smooth, R-2

106

Clear, 9.25", Top-Blob, Type-Blob, Bot-Smooth, R-2

ENGLE BOTTLING WORKS 'D'-Continued

107

Aqua, 9.75", Top-Blob, Type-Blob, Bot-Smooth, R-2, Panel Base, Lady Leg Neck

108

Apple Green, 9.50", Top-Blob, Type-Blob, Bot-Smooth, R-4, 13 Fl oz, the 1/2 oz etched out on rear

109

Amber, 9.75", Top-Blob, Type-Blob, Bot-Smooth, R-3, 13 1/2 Fl oz

110

Aqua, 9.50", Top-Blob, Type-Blob, Bot-Smooth, R-1, 13 Fl oz, 1/2 oz etched out on rear,

111

Aqua, 9.50", Top-Blob, Type-Blob, Bot-Smooth, R-1, no Net wt

112

Aqua, 9.50", Top-Blob, Type-Blob, Bot-Smooth, R-1, 13 1/2 Fl oz

ENGLE BOTTLING WORKS 'D'-Continued

113

Aqua, 9.75, Top-Crown, Type-Crown, Bot-Smooth, R-1, 13 1/2 Fl oz

114

Amber, 9.50", Top-Crown, Type-Crown, Bot-Smooth, R-6, Tan and Black label, stated as Rieker's White Label, Rieker Star Brewery logo, Rieker's brand beer, Engle Bottling Works, with P.P. Diehl, Prop.

ENTERPRISE BOTTLING SUPPLY CO. OF PA.

101

Aqua, 8.00", Top-Blob, type-Hutch, Bot-Smooth, R-3

102

Apple Green, 8.00", Top-Blob, type-Hutch, Bot-Smooth, R-3

103

Aqua, 8.00", Top-Blob, type-Hutch, Bot-Smooth, R-3

FREY, W. B.

101

Aqua, 6.75", Top-Blob, Type-Hutch, Bot-Smooth, R-5

102

Aqua, 9.25", Top-Blob, Type-Blob, Bot-Smooth, R-6

103

Clear, 9.25", Top-Blob, Type-Blob, Bot-Smooth, R-6

FULMER, A. P. (Aldus)

101

Olive Green, 9.50", Top-Applied Top, Type-Three Piece, Bot-Sand Pontil, R-5

GERSTLY, W. F.

101

Clear, 9.50", Top-Crown,
type-Crown, Bot-Smooth,
R-5

GIBSON, L. L.

101

Aqua, 9.25", Top-Blob,
Type-Blob, Bot-Smooth,
R-6

G/R (GEORGE E. REESE)

Please see George E. Reese below

GRIMECY, HARRY W.

101

Aqua, 9.50, Top-Blob, Type-Blob, Bot-Smooth, R-3

102

Clear, 9.50, Top-Blob, Type-Blob, Bot-Smooth, R-2, Very large horseshoe

103

Clear, 9.25, Top-Blob, Type-Blob, Bot-Smooth, R-2, Small horseshoe

104

Aqua, 9.75, Top-Blob, Type-Blob, Bot-Smooth, R-2, Panel base, Small horseshoe

105

Clear, 9.50, Top-Blob, Type-Blob, Bot-Smooth, R-2, Medium horseshoe

106

Aqua, 9.75, Top-Blob, Type-Blob, Bot-Smooth, R-2, Panel base, Small horseshoe, light 104 variant

GRIMECY, HARRY W. - Continued

107

Clear, 9.00, Top-Crown,
Type-Crown, Bot-Smooth,
R-2, Small horseshoe

108

Aqua, 9.75, Top-Blob, Type-Blob, Bot-Smooth, R-2, Panel base, Small horseshoe, Crown version of 104 & 106

109

Aqua, 9.50, Top-Crown,
Type-Crown, Bot-Smooth,
R-2, Medium horseshoe

110

Clear, 9.50, Top-Crown,
Type-Crown, Bot-Smooth,
R-2, similar slug to 101

HLF & CO. (Henry L. Franke)

101

Blue Green, 7.50", Top-Applied Top, Type Squat, Bot-Iron Pontil, R-5

102

Dark Green, 6.75", Top-Applied Top, Type-Squat, Bot-Iron Pontil, R-6

HAEFNER BREWING COMPANY

101

Amber, 9.50, Top-Crown, Type-Crown, Bot-Smooth, R-4

102

Amber, 9.50, Top-Crown, Type-Crown, Bot-Smooth, R-4

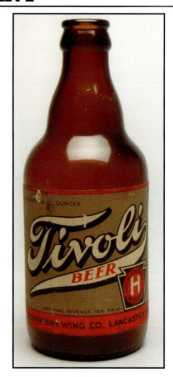

103

Amber, 7.00, Top-Crown, Type-Crown, Bot-Smooth, R-2

HAEFNER BREWING COMPANY - Continued

104

Clear, 7.00, Top-Crown, Type-Crown, Bot-Smooth, R-2

105

Clear, 9.50, Top-Crown, Type-Crown, Bot-Smooth, R-2

106

Clear, 9.50, Top-Crown, Type-Crown, Bot-Smooth, R-2

107

Clear, 9.50, Top-Crown, Type-Crown, Bot-Smooth, R-2

108

Clear, 9.50, Top-Crown, Type-Crown, Bot-Smooth, R-2

109

Amber, 9.50, Top-Crown, Type-Crown, Bot-Smooth, R-4

HAEFNER BREWING COMPANY - Continued

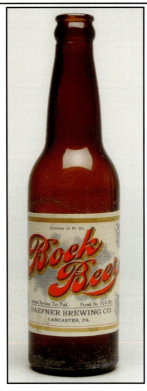

110

Amber, 9.50, Top-Crown, Type-Crown, Bot-Smooth, R-4

111

Amber, 9.50, Top-Crown, Type-Crown, Bot-Smooth, R-3

112

Amber, 9.50, Top-Crown, Type-Crown, Bot-Smooth, R-3

113

Clear, 9.50, Top-Crown, Type-Crown, Bot-Smooth, R-3

114

Clear, 9.50, Top-Crown, Type-Crown, Bot-Smooth, R-3, PRE PROHIBITION STRENGTH

115

Clear, 9.50, Top-Crown, Type-Crown, Bot-Smooth, R-3

HAEFNER BREWING COMPANY - Continued

116

Clear, 9.50, Top-Crown, Type-Crown, Bot-Smooth, R-3

117

Amber, 7.00, Top-Crown, Type-Crown, Bot-Smooth, R-1

118

Clear, 9.50, Top-Crown, Type-Crown, Bot-Smooth, R-3

119

Amber, 7.00, Top-Crown, Type-Crown, Bot-Smooth, R-3

120

Amber, 7.00, Top-Crown, Type-Crown, Bot-Smooth, R-3

121

Amber, 9.50, Top-Crown, Type-Crown, Bot-Smooth, R-3

HAEFNER BREWING COMPANY - Continued

122

Clear, 9.50, Top-Crown,
Type-Crown, Bot-Smooth,
R-4

123

Clear, 9.50, Top-Crown,
Type-Crown, Bot-Smooth,
R-4

124

Amber, 7.00, Top-Crown,
Type-Crown, Bot-Smooth,
R-4

125

Clear, 9.50, Top-Crown,
Type-Crown, Bot-Smooth,
R-5

126

Amber, 9.50, Top-Crown,
Type-Crown, Bot-Smooth,
R-5

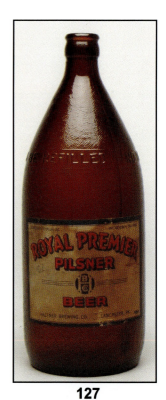

127

Amber, 9.50, Top-Crown,
Type-Crown, Bot-Smooth,
R-5

HAEFNER BREWING COMPANY - Continued

128

Clear, 9.50, Top-Crown,
Type-Crown, Bot-Smooth,
R-6, Bock label

129

Amber, 9.50, Top-Crown,
Type-Crown, Bot-Smooth,
R-6

130

Amber, 7.00, Top-Crown,
Type-Crown, Bot-Smooth,
R-6

131

Amber, 7.00, Top-Crown,
Type-Crown, Bot-Smooth,
R-6

HAIN, CHARLES

101

Clear, 9.50", Top-Blob, Type-Blob, Bot-Smooth, R-3

102

Aqua, 9.00", Top-Blob, Type-Blob, Bot-Smooth, R-2

103

Aqua, 9.25", Top-Blob, Type-Blob, Bot-Smooth, R-2

HAIN, CHARLES - Cont.   HALLMAN, H. C. (Harry)

104

Aqua, 9.25", Top-Blob, Type-Blob, Bot-Smooth, R-3, large letters on reverse

105

Aqua, 9.25", Top-Blob, Type-Blob, Bot-Smooth, R-3, small letters on reverse

101

Aqua, 6.75", Top-Blob, Type- Hutch, Bot-Smooth, R-5, Tombstone slug plate

HAMBRIGHT, W. A. HANBRIGHT, W. A. HAUS, B. F.

101

Clear, 9.50", Top-Blob, Type-Blob, Bot-Smooth, R-4

102

Aqua, 9.00", Top-Blob, Type-Blob, Bot-Smooth, R-5, misspelled version of Hambright on left

101

Aqua, 7.25", Top-Applied Top, Type-Squat, Bot-Iron Pontil, R-6, extremely rare bottle

HYGRADE BOTTLING WORKS

101

Clear, 9.00", Top-Crown, Type-Crown, Bot-Smooth, R-2

102

Aqua, 9.50", Top-Crown, Type-Crown, Bot-Smooth, R-2

HYGRADE BOTTLING WORKS - Continued

103

Clear, 9.00", Top-Crown, Type-Crown, Bot-Smooth, R-2

104

Aqua, 9.00", Top-Crown, Type-Crown, Bot-Smooth, R-2

105

Aqua, 9.25", Top-Crown, Type-Crown, Bot-Smooth, R-3

106

Clear, 8.75", Top-Crown, Type-Crown, Bot-Smooth, R-4

INGLESIDE BOTTLING WORKS

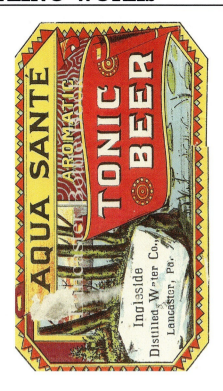

101

Aqua, 6.50", Top-Blob,
Type-Hutch, Bot-Smooth,
R-2

Rear label for variant 101, R-6; was placed
on the unembossed portion of bottle, similar
to Geo A Keihl 106-Rear

102

Aqua, 9.25", Top-Blob,
Type-Blob, Bot-Smooth,
R-3

103

Aqua, 9.50", Top-Blob,
Type-Blob, Bot-Smooth,
R-2

104

Clear, 9.25", Top-Blob,
Type-Blob, Bot-Smooth,
R-5

J/S, SCHWENDE, J.

Please see Schwende, J.

KEEFER, W. W.

101

Aqua, 9.75", Top-Crown, Type-Crown, Bot-Smooth, R-4, although on a larger bottle, the label states only 6.5 fl oz.

102

Aqua, 9.50", Top-Crown, Type-Crown, Bot-Smooth, R-1

103

Aqua, 9.75", Top-Crown, Type-Crown, Bot-Smooth, R-1

104

Aqua, 9.50", Top-Crown, Type-Crown, Bot-Smooth, R-1

105

Amber, 9.25", Top-Crown, Type-Crown, Bot-Smooth, R-1

106

Amber, 9.25", Top-Crown, Type-Crown, Bot-Smooth, R-1

KEEFER, W. W. - Continued

107

Aqua, 7.50", Top-Crown, Type-Crown, Bot-Smooth, R-1

108

Aqua, 7.75", Top-Crown, Type-Crown, Bot-Smooth, R-1

109

Clear, 8.50", Top-Crown, Type-Crown, Bot-Smooth, R-1, lace pattern

KEGEL, H. J.

101

Aqua, 9.00", Top-Blob, Type-Blob, Bot-Smooth, R-6, large horseshoe

KIEHL, GEORGE A.

101

Blue Green, 6.50", Top-Double Taper, type-Squat, Bot-Smooth, R-5

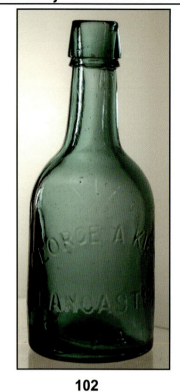

102

Med Green, 6.50", Top-Double Taper, type-Squat, Bot-Smooth, R-4

103

Aqua, Top-Applied Top, Type-Hutch, Bot-Smooth, R-7, rare shape, tombstone slug

104

Aqua, 7.25", Top-Applied Top, Type-Gravitating Stopper, Bot-Smooth, R-4

105

Aqua, 7.25, Top-Applied Top, Type-Squat, Bot-Smooth, R-2

106

Amber, 6.50", Top-Blob, Type-Hutch, Bot-Smooth, R-6, extremely rare color

KIEHL, GEORGE A. - Continued

106 - Rear

Ginger Ale label on reverse side of Variant 106

107

Dark Amber, 6.50", Top-Blob, Type-Hutch, Bot-Smooth, R-6

108

Aqua, 6.75", Top-Blob, Type-Hutch, Bot-Smooth, R-1

109

Apple Green, 6.75", Top-Blob, Type-Hutch, Bot-Smooth, R-3, also states & Co.

110

Aqua, 6.75", Top-Blob, Type-Hutch, Bot-Smooth, R-1, also states & Co.

111

Aqua, 8.25", Top-Applied Top, Type-Codds, Bot-Smooth, R-4

KIEHL, GEORGE A. - Continued

112

Aqua, 7.75", Top-Applied Top, Type-Codds, Bot-Smooth, R-3, with cobalt blue marble

113

A third Codds variant is known to exist, no photo is available, smaller slug

114

Aqua, 8.00", Top-Blob, Type-16 oz. Hutch, Bot-Smooth, R-6, extremely rare size

115

Clear, 8.00", Top-Blob, Type-16- oz. Hutch, Bot-Smooth, R-6, extremely rare size

116

Apple Green, 8.75", Top-Blob, Type-Blob, Bot-Smooth, R-6, extremely rare color

KIEHL, GEORGE A. - Continued

117
Aqua, 9.25", Top-Blob,
Type-Blob, Bot-Smooth,
R-1

118
Aqua, 9.00", Top-Blob,
Type-Blob, Bot-Smooth,
R-1

119
Aqua, 9.25", Top-Blob,
Type-Blob, Bot-Smooth,
R-1

120
Aqua, 9.25", Top-Blob,
Type-Blob, Bot-Smooth,
R-1

KIEHL, GEORGE A. - Continued

121

Aqua, 9.25", Top-Blob, Type-Blob, Bot-Smooth, R-1

122

Aqua, 9.25", Top-Blob, Type-Blob, Bot-Smooth, R-1

123

Clear, 9.50", Top-Blob, Type-Blob, Bot-Smooth, R-1

KIEHL & KEEFER

101

Aqua, 6.50", Top-Blob, Type-Hutch, Bot-Smooth, R-2

102

Aqua, 6.50", Top-Blob, Type-Hutch, Bot-Smooth, R-1

103

Clear, 6.50", Top-Blob, Type-Hutch, Bot-Smooth, R-3

KIEHL & KEEFER - Continued

104

Aqua, 9.25", Top-Blob, Type-Blob, Bot-Smooth, R-4

105

Aqua, 9.25", Top-Blob, Type-Blob, Bot-Smooth, R-1, See reference to Reiker 104

106

Aqua, 8.75", Top-Blob, Type-Blob, Bot-Smooth, R-2

107

Clear, 9.75", Top-Blob, Type-Blob, Bot-Smooth, R-3

108

Clear, 9.50", Top-Blob, Type-Blob, Bot-Smooth, R-2

109

Clear, 8.75", Top-Blob, Type-Blob, Bot-Smooth, R-2

KIEHL & KEEFER - Continued

110

Aqua, 8.75", Top-Blob, Type-Blob, Bot-Smooth, R-4

111

Clear, 9.50", Top-Blob, Type-Blob, Bot-Smooth, R-5, Lady Leg Neck, Panel Base, Label reads Bartholomay Brewery Co. Rochester Gilt Edge

112

Clear, 9.75", Top-Blob, Type-Blob, Bot-Smooth, R-1, Lady Leg Neck, Panel Base

113

Aqua, 9.75", Top-Blob, Type-Blob, Bot-Smooth, R-1, Lady Leg Neck, Panel Base

114

Aqua, 9.25", Top-Blob, Type-Blob, Bot-Smooth, R-1, Lady Leg Neck, Panel Base

115

Amber, 9.00", Top-Blob, Type-Blob, Bot-Smooth, R-1, Lady Leg Neck, Panel Base

KIEHL & KEEFER - Continued

116

Amber, 9.00", Top-Blob, Type-Blob, Bot-Smooth, R-1, Lady Leg Neck, Panel Base, 1903 on base rear

117

Aqua, 7.50", Top-Blob, Type-Blob, Bot-Smooth, R-1

118

Aqua, 7.75", Top-Blob, Type-Blob, Bot-Smooth, R-1

119

Aqua, 7.75", Top-Blob, Type-Blob, Bot-Smooth, R-1

120

Clear, 8.00", Top-Blob, Type-Blob, Bot-Smooth, R-1

121

Aqua, 9.50", Top-Blob, Type-Blob, Bot-Smooth, R-1

KIEHL & KEEFER - Continued

122

Aqua, 9.50", Top-Crown, Type-Crown, Bot-Smooth, R-1, Lady Leg Neck, Panel Base

123

Amber, 9.75", Top-Crown, Type-Crown, Bot-Smooth, R-3, Lady Leg Neck, Panel Base

124

Amber, 9.25", Top-Crown, Type-Crown, Bot-Smooth, R-1

125

Amber, 9.25", Top-Crown, Type-Crown, Bot-Smooth, R-1

126

Amber, 9.25", Top-Crown, Type-Crown, Bot-Smooth, R-1

KIEHL & KEEFER - Continued

127

Identical to variant 126,
except Schlitz on bottom,
R-4

128

Aqua, 7.75", Top-Crown,
Type-Crown, Bot-Smooth,
R-1

KIEHL & KEEFER - Schlitz

Schlitz embossed on bottom, authors believe this has some relationship to the Schlitz wholesale operation by Harry Grimecy.

KIEHL & WACKER

101

Blue Green, 6.75", Top-
Double Taper, Type-Squat,
Bot-Iron Pontil, R-4

102-Front

Dark Green, 7.25", Top-
Applied Top, Type-Squat,
Bot-Iron Pontil, R-5

102-Rear

Mineral Water on reverse

KIEHL & WACKER - Continued

103

Light Green, 6.50", Top-Double Taper, Type-Squat, Bot-Smooth, R-3

104

Aqua, 6.50", Top-Double Taper, Type-Squat, Bot-Smooth, R-3

105

Apple Green, 6.50", Top-Double Taper, Type-Squat, Bot-Smooth, R-6

106-Front

Aqua, 7.00", Top-Applied Top, Type-Squat, Bot-Smooth, R-5

KIEHL & WACKER - Continued

106-Rear

Mineral Water on rear

107

Aqua, 7.25", Top-Applied Top, Type-Squat, Bot-Smooth, R-3

108

Apple Green, 6.50", Top-Double Taper, Type-Squat, Bot-Iron Pontil, R-6

KIST BOTTLING COMPANY

101

Clear, 11.75", Top-Crown, Type-Soft Drink, Bot-Smooth, R-1

102

Clear, 8.00", Top-Crown, Type-Soft Drink, Bot-Smooth, R-1

103

Mod Green, 11.75", Top-Crown, Type-Soft Drink, Bot-Smooth, R-2

KLUGH, ADAM M.   KRIMMEL, AUGUST

101

Clear, 7.75", Top-Blob,
Type-Pony, Bot-Smooth,
R-6, extremely rare

101

Aqua, 6.50", Top-Blob,
Type-Hutch, Bot-Smooth,
R-3, medium horseshoe

102

Clear, 9.50", Top-Blob,
Type-Blob, Bot-Smooth,
R-2, medium horseshoe

103

Clear, 9.25", Top-Blob,
Type-Blob, Bot-Smooth,
R-2, large horseshoe

104

Aqua, 9.00", Top-Blob,
Type-Blob, Bot-Smooth,
R-2, large horseshoe

105

Aqua, 9.00", Top-Blob,
Type-Blob, Bot-Smooth,
R-4, large horseshoe

LANCASTER BOTTLING COMPANY - C. G. BATES & SON, MGRS

101

Clear, 9.50", Top-Blob,
Type-Blob, Bot-Smooth,
R-6

LANCASTER BOTTLING COMPANY

101

Modern Green, 8.50", Top-Crown, Type-Soft Drink,
Bot-Smooth, R-2, "Gold Arrow", Prototype bottle,
per interview with daughter of Ab Karlip, owner

102

Clear, 8.50", Top-Crown,
Type-Soft Drink, Bot-
Smooth, R-1

LANCASTER BOTTLING COMPANY - Continued

103

Modern Green, 8.50", Top-Crown, Type-Soft Drink, Bot-Smooth, R-1, "White Arrow"

104

Clear, 8.25, Top-Crown, Type-Soft Drink, Bot-Smooth, R-1, white & red pyro, Red Rock Brand

105

Clear, 9.75, Top-Crown, Type-Soft Drink, Bot-Smooth, R-1, white & red pyro, Red Rock Brand

106

Clear, 8.25, Top-Crown, Type-Soft Drink, Bot-Smooth, R-1, white & red pyro, Red Rock Brand

107

Clear, 9.75, Top-Crown, Type-Soft Drink, Bot-Smooth, R-1, white & red pyro, Red Rock Brand

LANCASTER BOTTLING COMPANY - Continued

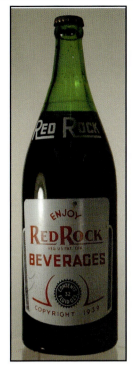

108

Modern Green, 11.75, Top-Crown, Type-Soft Drink, Bot-Smooth, R-1, white & red pyro, Red Rock brand

109

Clear, 11.75, Top-Crown, Type-Soft Drink, Bot-Smooth, R-1, white & red pyro, Red Rock brand

110

Identical to 109, R-2, but no pyro label, embossing on bottom, also LEA and 3 ribs on neck, most likely had a paper label

111

Modern Green, 9.50", Top-Crown, Type-Soft Drink, Bot-Smooth, R-2

112

Clear, Top-9.75", Top-Crown, Type-Soft Drink, Bot-Smooth, R-2

LANCASTER BOTTLING COMPANY - Continued

113

Clear, 8.75", Top-Crown, Type-Soft Drink, Bot-Smooth, R-1, checkerboard, Conestoga Beverages diagonally

114

Identical to 109, Modern Green, R-2, red & white pyro label, embossing on bottom, also LEA and 3 ribs on neck

LANCASTER BOTTLING WORKS

101

Clear, 9.75", Top-Blob, Type-Blob, Bot-Smooth, R-6, Lady Leg Neck, Panel Base

LANCASTER BREWERY, INC. (OLD)

101

Amber, 9.50", Top-Crown, Type-Crown, Bot-Smooth, R-3

102

Same as 101, except vertical writing on left side of label, R-4

103

Amber, 9.50", Top-Crown, Type-Crown, Bot-Smooth, R-4

LANC. BREW. INC. (OLD) LANC. BREW. CO. (MODERN)

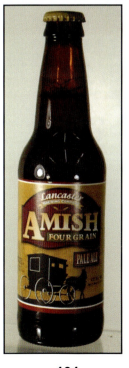

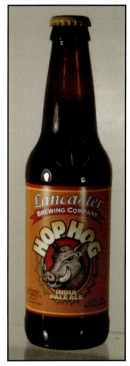

104

Amber, 9.50", Top-Crown, Type-Crown, Bot-Smooth, R-5

101

Amber, 9.00, Top-Crown, Type-Crown, Bot-Smooth, R-1

102

Amber, 9.00, Top-Crown, Type-Crown, Bot-Smooth, R-1

LANCASTER BREWING COMPANY (MODERN) - Cont.

103

Amber, 9.00, Top-Crown, Type-Crown, Bot-Smooth, R-1

104

Amber, 9.00, Top-Crown, Type-Crown, Bot-Smooth, R-2, discontinued

105

Amber, 9.00, Top-Crown, Type-Crown, Bot-Smooth, R-1

106

Amber, 9.00, Top-Crown, Type-Crown, Bot-Smooth, R-1

107

Amber, 9.00, Top-Crown, Type-Crown, Bot-Smooth, R-3, Lancaster Barnstormers - All Star Game Bottle

108

Amber, 9.00, Top-Crown, Type-Crown, Bot-Smooth, R-1

LANCASTER BREWING COMPANY (MODERN) - Continued

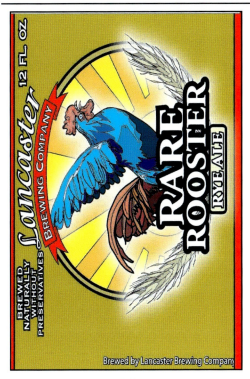

109
Prototype label, for upcoming release of new product, R-6

110
Amber, 12.50, Top-Wire Clasp, Type-Growler, Bot-Smooth, R-1

111
Mod Green, 12.50, Top-Wire Clasp, Type-Growler, Bot-Smooth, R-2

112
Amber, 12.50, Top-Wire Clasp, Type-Growler, Bot-Smooth, R-7, Prototype

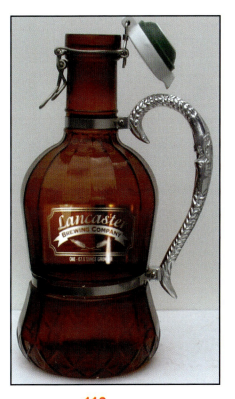

113
Amber, 12.50, Top-Wire Clasp, Type-Growler, Bot-Smooth, R-7, Prototype

114
Amber, 9.00, Top-Crown, Type-Crown, Bot-Smooth, R-1

LANCASTER MALT BREWING COMPANY

101

Amber, 9.00, Top-Crown, Type-Crown, Bot-Smooth, R-7, unique prototype label

102

Amber, 9.00, Top-Crown, Type-Crown, Bot-Smooth, R-1

103

Amber, 9.00, Top-Crown, Type-Crown, Bot-Smooth, R-1

104

Amber, 9.00, Top-Crown, Type-Crown, Bot-Smooth, R-1

105

Amber, 9.00, Top-Crown, Type-Crown, Bot-Smooth, R-1

106

Amber, 9.00, Top-Crown, Type-Crown, Bot-Smooth, R-1

LANCASTER MALT BREWING COMPANY - Continued

107

Amber, 9.00, Top-Crown, Type-Crown, Bot-Smooth, R-1

108

Amber, 9.00, Top-Crown, Type-Crown, Bot-Smooth, R-1

109

Amber, 9.00, Top-Crown, Type-Crown, Bot-Smooth, R-1

110

Amber, 9.00, Top-Crown, Type-Crown, Bot-Smooth, R-1

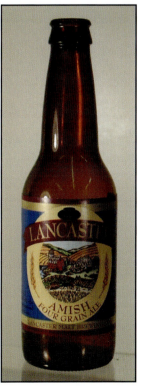

111

Amber, 9.00, Top-Crown, Type-Crown, Bot-Smooth, R-1

LANCASTER MALT BREWING COMPANY - Continued

112

Amber, 9.00, Top-Crown, Type-Crown, Bot-Smooth, R-1

113

Clear, 10.50, Top-Screw, Type-Growler, Bot-Smooth, R-1

MCGRANN, MICHAEL (Michl)

101

Blue Green, 6.75", Top-Double-Taper, Type-Squat, Bot-Iron Pontil, R-3

102

Dark Olive Green, 6.50", Top-Double-Taper, Type-Squat, Bot-Smooth, R-4

MCGRANN, MICHAEL (Michl)

103

Med Green, 6.50", Top-Double-Taper, Type-Squat, Bot-Iron Pontil, R-3

104

Med Green, 6.50", Top-Double-Taper, Type-Squat, Bot-Smooth, R-3

METROPOLITAN BOTTLING WORKS

101

Clear, 9.75, Top-Crown, Type-Crown, Bot-Smooth, R-5, 249 North Queen Street embossed on front of bottle

102

Amber, 9.50, Top-Crown, Type-Crown, Bot-Smooth, R-5, 249 North Queen Street embossed on front of bottle

METZGER BROS.

101

Aqua, 9.75", Top-Blob, Type-Blob, Bot-Smooth, R-4

MIL-CO

101

Clear, 7.25, Top-Crown, Type-Soft Drink, Bot-Smooth, R-5

MILLER, PHILLIP H.

101

Clear, 9.25, Top-Blob, Type-Blob, Bot-Smooth, R-2

102

Aqua, 9.00, Top-Blob, Type-Blob, Bot-Smooth, R-2

NEHI BOTTLING COMPANY

101

Clear, 9.75", Top-Crown, Type-Soft Drink, Bot-Smooth, R-3, entire bottle embossed in pattern

NORBECK, GEO S. (George)

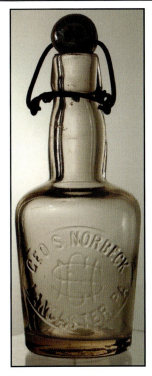

101
Clear, 6.75", Top-Blob, Type-Pony, Bot-Smooth, R-5

102
Clear, 9.25", Top-Blob, Type-Blob, Bot-Smooth, R-2

103
Clear, 9.25", Top-Blob, Type-Blob, Bot-Smooth, R-2

104
Clear, 9.25", Top-Blob, Type-Blob, Bot-Smooth, R-3

105
Amber, 9.25", Top-Blob, Type-Blob, Bot-Smooth, R-7, unique, no embossing

105-Label
R-7, Wurzburger, Hofbrau Beer, notice King Street and Grant Street addresses and Norbeck Bottling Works name

OLDE LANCASTER BREWING COMPANY

101

Amber, 7.00, Top-Crown, Type-Crown, Bot-Smooth, R-1

102

Amber, 7.00, Top-Crown, Type-Crown, Bot-Smooth, R-1

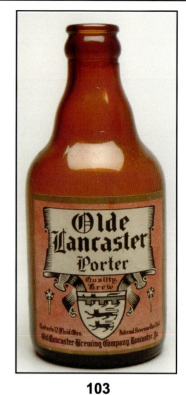

103

Amber, 7.00, Top-Crown, Type-Crown, Bot-Smooth, R-1

104

Amber, 7.00, Top-Crown, Type-Crown, Bot-Smooth, R-1

105

Amber, 7.00, Top-Crown, Type-Crown, Bot-Smooth, R-1

106

Amber, 7.00, Top-Crown, Type-Crown, Bot-Smooth, R-1

OLDE LANCASTER BREWING COMPANY - Continued

107

Amber, 7.00, Top-Crown, Type-Crown, Bot-Smooth, R-3

108

Amber, 9.75, Top-Crown, Type-Crown, Bot-Smooth, R-1

109

Amber, 7.00, Top-Crown, Type-Crown, Bot-Smooth, R-1

110

Amber, 12.00, Top-Crown, Type-Crown, Bot-Smooth, R-3, embossed

111

Amber, 12.00, Top-Crown, Type-Crown, Bot-Smooth, R-3, embossed

112

Amber, 12.00, Top-Crown, Type-Crown, Bot-Smooth, R-3

PENN STAR BREWERY

101

Clear, 9.50, Top-Crown, Type-Crown, Bot-Smooth, R-1, was first label, notice Ref. to Rieker's

102

Clear, 9.50, Top-Crown, Type-Crown, Bot-Smooth, R-2

103

Clear, 9.50, Top-Crown, Type-Crown, Bot-Smooth, R-2

104

Clear, 9.50, Top-Crown, Type-Crown, Bot-Smooth, R-2

105

Amber, 12.00, Top-Crown, Type-Crown, Bot-Smooth, R-3

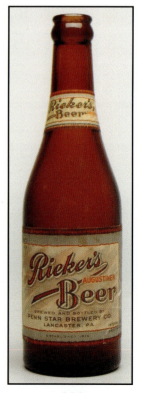

106

Amber, 9.50, Top-Crown, Type-Crown, Bot-Smooth, R-2

PENN STAR BREWERY - Continued

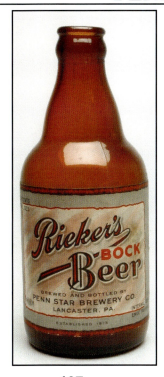

107

Amber, 7.00, Top-Crown, Type-Crown, Bot-Smooth, R-2

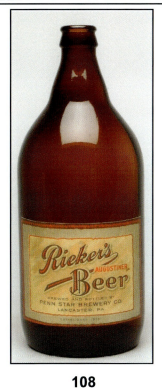

108

Amber, 9.75, Top-Crown, Type-Crown, Bot-Smooth, R-3

109

Clear, 9.50, Top-Crown, Type-Crown, Bot-Smooth, R-2

110

Clear, 9.50, Top-Crown, Type-Crown, Bot-Smooth, R-2, notice ref. to both Penn Star & Penn State

111

Clear, 9.50, Top-Crown, Type-Crown, Bot-Smooth, R-2

112

Amber, 9.75, Top-Crown, Type-Crown, Bot-Smooth, R-3

PENN STATE BREWERY

101

Clear, 9.50, Top-Crown, Type-Crown, Bot-Smooth, R-1, first label, notice Ref. to Rieker's, also notice similar color & style to Penn Star 101

102

Amber, 12.00, Top-Crown, Type-Crown, Bot-Smooth, R-2

103

Amber, 12.00, Top-Crown, Type-Crown, Bot-Smooth, R-2

104

Amber, 12.00, Top-Crown, Type-Crown, Bot-Smooth, R-2

105

Clear, 9.50, Top-Crown, Type-Crown, Bot-Smooth, R-2

106

Amber, 7.00, Top-Crown, Type-Crown, Bot-Smooth, R-4, High Test

PENN STATE BREWERY - Continued

107

Clear, 9.50, Top-Crown,
Type-Crown, Bot-Smooth,
R-2

108

Amber, 7.00, Top-Crown,
Type-Crown, Bot-Smooth,
R-4, High Test

109

Amber, 9.75, Top-Crown,
Type-Crown, Bot-Smooth,
R-2

110

Amber, 7.00, Top-Crown,
Type-Crown, Bot-Smooth,
R-2

111

Clear, 9.50, Top-Crown,
Type-Crown, Bot-Smooth,
R-2

PONTZ, JOHN (JNO)

101

Aqua, 6.50", Top-Blob, Type-Hutch, Bot-Smooth, R-3

102

Aqua, 9.25", Top-Blob, Type-Blob, Bot-Smooth, R-2, JNO for John, no embossing on rear

103

Aqua, 9.25", Top-Blob, Type-Blob, Bot-Smooth, R-2

104

Clear, 9.25", Top-Blob, Type-Blob, Bot-Smooth, R-3

105

Aqua, 9.25", Top-Blob, Type-Blob, Bot-Smooth, R-2, JNO for John, This Bottle Not To Be Sold, small on rear

106

Aqua, 9.25", Top-Blob, Type-Blob, Bot-Smooth, R-2, JNO for John, This Bottle Not To Be Sold, large on rear

PURE BEVERAGE CO.

101

Aqua, 9.75", Top-Crown, Type-Soft Drink, Bot-Smooth, R-1

102

Clear, 8.50", Top-Crown, Type-Soft Drink, Bot-Smooth, R-1, 8-sided panel embossing

QUADE, F. (Frederick)

101

Dark Amber, 9.00", Top-Blob, Type-Blob, Bot-Smooth, R-5

102

Aqua, 9.00", Top-Blob, Type-Blob, Bot-Smooth, R-4

103

Aqua, 9.00", Top-Blob, Type-Blob, Bot-Smooth, R-4

QUADE, F. (Frederick) - Continued

104
Aqua, 9.00", Top-Blob, Type-Blob, Bot-Smooth, R-5

104
Honey Amber, 9.00", Top-Blob, Type-Blob, Bot-Smooth, R-6

REESE, GEORGE E.

101
Aqua, 6.50", Top-Blob-Type-Hutch, Bot-Smooth, R-4, Tombstone Slug

102
Clear, 6.50", Top-Blob-Type-Hutch, Bot-Smooth, R-2

103
Clear, 9.25", Top-Blob, Type-Blob, Bot-Smooth, R-4

REESE, GEORGE E. - Continued

104

Clear, 9.25", Top-Blob, Type-Blob, Bot-Smooth, R-4, 524 Manor St. on slug

105

Clear, 9.75", Top-Blob, Type-Blob, Bot-Smooth, R-3

106

Clear, 9.75", Top-Blob, Type-Blob, Bot-Smooth, R-3, similar to variant 105, but larger. This Bottle Not To Be Sold

107

Clear, 9.25", Top-Blob, Type-Blob, Bot-Smooth, R-2

108

Clear, 9.50", Top-Blob, Type-Blob, Bot-Smooth, R-4, Lancaster misspelled Lancasater

109

Clear, 9.50", Top-Blob, Type-Blob, Bot-Smooth, R-2

G/R (George E. Reese)

Please see George E. Reese.

RIEKER, FRANK A.

101
Aqua, 9.50", Top-Blob, Type-Blob, Bot-Smooth, R-5, most ornate embossed Lancaster bottle, was made as a Christmas give away

102
Aqua, 9.25", Top-Blob, Type-Blob, Bot-Smooth, R-6, fat blob

103
Aqua, 9.75", Top-Blob, Type-Blob, Bot-Smooth, R-6, This Bottle Never To Be Sold on rear

FRANK A. RIEKER   RUTTGERS WEISS BIER, C. (Constantine)

104
Aqua, 9.50", Top-Blob, Type-Blob, Bot-Smooth, R-7, Extremely rare Frank A. Reiker label on Kiehl & Keefer 105 bottle

101
Aqua, 7.50", Top-Blob, Type-Blob, Bot-Smooth, R-6, width of bottle is 3", very unusual shape

SCHAEFFER, A. B. (Alfred)

101

Clear, 9.50", Top-Blob,
Type-Blob, Bot-Smooth,
R-6, rare

SCHMIDT, J. & CO.

101

Clear, 9.00", Top-Blob,
Type-Blob, Bot-Smooth,
R-4

102

Aqua, 9.00", Top-Blob, Type-Blob,
Bot-Smooth, R-5, J. Schmitt & Co.
embossed vertically in scroll,

SCHMITT & BEILMAN

101

Clear, 9.25", Top-Blob, Type-Blob, Bot-Smooth, R-3

102

Aqua, 9.00", Top-Blob, Type-Blob, Bot-Smooth, R-3

103

Aqua, 9.25", Top-Blob, Type-Blob, Bot-Smooth, R-3

104

Aqua, 9.00", Top-Blob, Type-Blob, Bot-Smooth, R-7, misspelled word "bottlers" on front missing the R

105

Clear, 9.25", Top-Blob, Type-Blob, Bot-Smooth, R-3

106

Clear, 9.25", Top-Blob, Type-Blob, Bot-Smooth, R-3

SCHWENDE, J.

101

Clear, 9.50", Top-Blob, Type-Blob, Bot-Smooth, R-4

102

Aqua, 8.75", Top-Blob, Type-Blob, Bot-Smooth, R-4

103

Aqua, 9.25", Top-Blob, Type-Blob, Bot-Smooth, R-1

104

Aqua, 9.25", Top-Blob, Type-Blob, Bot-Smooth, R-1

105

Aqua, 9.00", Top-Crown, Type-Crown, Bot-Smooth, R-1

106

Apple Green, 9.50", Top-Crown, Type-Crown, Bot-Smooth, R-1

SCHWENDE, J. - (Cont.)   SEVEN UP BOTTLING COMPANY

107
Aqua, 9.50", Top-Crown, Type-Crown, Bot-Smooth, R-3

101
Clear, 9.50" Top-Crown, Type-Soft Drink, Bot-Smooth, R-1, green and white pyro Sno-Maid brand

102
Clear, 8.00" Top-Crown, Type-Soft Drink, Bot-Smooth, R-1, green and white pyro Sno-Maid brand

SHADEL (Charles)

101
Clear, 9.50", Top-Blob, Type-Blob, Bot-Smooth, R-6

102
Clear, 9.50", Top-Blob, Type-Blob, Bot-Smooth, R-4, This Bottle Not To Be Sold on bottom front

103
Clear, 9.00", Top-Blob, Type-Blob, Bot-Smooth, R-4, This Bottle Not To Be Sold on rear

SPRENGER BOTTLER

101

Aqua, 9.50", Top-Blob,
Type-Blob, Bot-Smooth,
R-3

102

Aqua, 9.25", Top-Blob,
Type-Blob, Bot-Smooth,
R-3

SPRENGER BREWING COMPANY

101

Aqua, 9.00", Top-Blob,
Type-Blob, Bot-Smooth,
R-4

102

Amber, 9.50", Top-Blob,
Type-Blob, Bot-Smooth,
R-2

103

Aqua, 9.00", Top-Blob,
Type-Blob, Bot-Smooth,
R-3

SPRENGER BREWING COMPANY - Continued

104

Aqua, 9.25", Top-Blob, Type-Blob, Bot-Smooth, R-2

105

Clear, 9.50", Top-Blob, Type-Blob, Bot-Smooth, R-2

106

Amber, 9.50", Top-Crown, Type-Crown, Bot-Smooth, R-2

107

Aqua, 9.50", Top-Crown, Type-Crown, Bot-Smooth, R-3

108

Clear, 9.50", Top-Crown, Type-Crown, Bot-Smooth, R-2

109

Amber, 9.50, Top-Crown, Type-Crown, Bot-Smooth, R-5

SPRENGER BREWING COMPANY - Continued

110

Amber, 9.50, Top-Crown, Type-Crown, Bot-Smooth, R-5

111

Amber, 9.50, Top-Crown, Type-Crown, Bot-Smooth, R-5

112

Amber, 9.50, Top-Crown, Type-Crown, Bot-Smooth, R-5

113

Amber, 9.50, Top-Crown, Type-Crown, Bot-Smooth, R-2

114

Clear, 9.50, Top-Crown, Type-Crown, Bot-Smooth, R-2

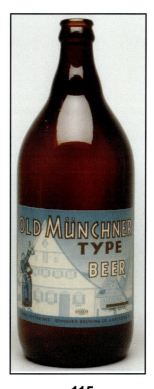

115

Amber, 9.75, Top-Crown, Type-Crown, Bot-Smooth, R-2, crossed out line of type

SPRENGER BREWING COMPANY - Continued

116

Amber, 9.75, Top-Crown,
Type-Crown, Bot-Smooth, R-2,
no crossed out lines of type

117-Front

Amber, 11.75, Type-Quart,
Top-Crown, Bot-Smooth,
R-1, embossed on bottom

117-Bottom

118

Amber, 11.75, Top-Crown,
Type-Crown, Bot-Smooth,
R-1

119

Amber, 11.75, Top-Crown,
Type-Crown, Bot-Smooth,
R-1

120

Clear, 9.50, Top-Crown,
Type-Crown, Bot-Smooth,
R-1

SPRENGER BREWING COMPANY - Continued

121

Clear, 9.50, Top-Crown, Type-Crown, Bot-Smooth, R-1

122

Clear, 9.50, Top-Crown, Type-Crown, Bot-Smooth, R-4, High Powered

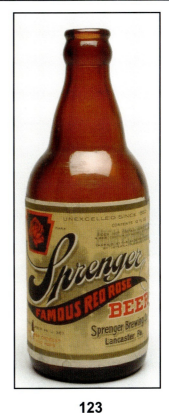

123

Amber, 7.00, Top-Crown, Type-Crown, Bot-Smooth, R-1

124

Amber, 7.00, Top-Crown, Type-Crown, Bot-Smooth, R-1, stamp on bottom of label

125

Amber, 7.00, Top-Crown, Type-Crown, Bot-Smooth, R-1

126

Amber, 7.00, Top-Crown, Type-Crown, Bot-Smooth, R-1

SPRENGER BREWING COMPANY - Continued

127

Amber, 7.00, Top-Crown, Type-Crown, Bot-Smooth, R-1, stamp on bottom of label

128

Amber, 7.00, Top-Crown, Type-Crown, Bot-Smooth, R-1, no Int Rev stamp

129

Amber, 7.00, Top-Crown, Type-Crown, Bot-Smooth, R-1

130

Amber, 9.75, Top-Crown, Type-Crown, Bot-Smooth, R-1

131

Clear, 9.50, Top-Crown, Type-Crown, Bot-Smooth, R-1, no Int rev stamp

132

Clear, 9.50, Top-Crown, Type-Crown, Bot-Smooth, R-1, Int Rev stamp

SPRENGER BREWING COMPANY - Continued

133

Amber, 9.75, Top-Crown, Type-Crown, Bot-Smooth, R-1

134

Clear, 9.50, Top-Crown, Type-Crown, Bot-Smooth, R-1

135

Clear, 9.50, Top-Crown, Type-Crown, Bot-Smooth, R-1, blanked out type in upper right of label

137

Green, 9.50, Top-Crown, Type-Crown, Bot-Smooth, R-1

138

Clear, 9.50, Top-Crown, Type-Crown, Bot-Smooth, R-1, blanked out text in lower left

139

Clear, 9.50, Top-Crown, Type-Crown, Bot-Smooth, R-1

SPRENGER BREWING COMPANY - Continued

140
Amber, 9.75, Top-Crown, Type-Crown, Bot-Smooth, R-1

141
Clear, 9.50, Top-Crown, Type-Crown, Bot-Smooth, R-1

137
Modern Green, 7.00, Top-Crown, Type-Crown, Bot-Smooth, R-1

138
Modern Green, 7.00, Top-Crown, Type-Crown, Bot-Smooth, R-1, stamp on lower left

140
Amber, 7.00, Top-Crown, Type-Crown, Bot-Smooth, R-1

141
Amber, 7.00, Top-Crown, Type-Crown, Bot-Smooth, R-1, blanked out text on upper right

SPRENGER BREWING COMPANY - Continued

143
Amber, 9.50, Top-Crown,
Type-Crown, Bot-Smooth,
R-3

144
Amber, 9.50, Top-Crown,
Type-Crown, Bot-Smooth,
R-3

THE SPRENGER CO.

101
Amber, 9.25", Top-Crown,
Type-Crown, Bot-Smooth,
R-2

SPRENGER, E. E. (Elizabeth)

101

Aqua, 6.75", Top-Blob, Type-Hutch, Bot-Smooth, R-3

102

Aqua, 6.75", Top-Blob, Type-Hutch, Bot-Smooth, R-4

103

Aqua, 6.50", Top-Blob, Type-Hutch, Bot-Smooth, R-3, panel base

104

Aqua, 9.25", Top-Blob, Type-Blob, Bot-Smooth, R-2

105

Clear, 9.25", Top-Blob, Type-Blob, Bot-Smooth, R-6, misspelled Sprenger as Springer

106

Aqua, 9.00", Top-Blob, Type-Blob, Bot-Smooth, R-2

SPRENGER, E. E. (Elizabeth)

107
Aqua, 9.00", Top-Blob,
Type-Blob, Bot-Smooth,
R-2

108
Aqua, 9.00", Top-Blob,
Type-Blob, Bot-Smooth,
R-2

SPRENGER, G. F. (George)

101
Aqua, 6.50", Top-Blob,
Type-Hutch, Bot-Smooth,
R-2, tombstone slug

102
Aqua, 6.50", Top-Blob,
Type-Hutch, Bot-Smooth,
R-2, tombstone slug

103
Aqua, 6.50", Top-Blob, Type-Hutch, Bot-Smooth, R-5, round slug, reverse N in Lancaster

SPRENGER, G. F. (George) - Continued

104

Aqua, 9.25", Top-Blob, Type-Quart Hutch, Bot-Smooth, R-6, tombstone slug

105

Aqua, 9.00", Top-Blob, Type-Quart Hutch, Bot-Smooth, R-6, round slug

106

Aqua, 9.00, Top-Blob, Type-Blob, Bot-Smooth, R-1

107

Aqua, 9.00, Top-Blob, Type-Blob, Bot-Smooth, R-1

108

Aqua, 9.25, Top-Blob, Type-Blob, Bot-Smooth, R-1

109

Amber, 6.50", Top-Blob, Type-Hutch, Bot-Smooth, R-6, extremely rare color

SPRENGER, J. A.

101

Aqua, 7.00", Top-Blob, Type-Squat, Bot-Smooth, R-7, Large star on slug

102

Aqua, 9.00", Top-Blob, Type-Blob, Bot-Smooth, R-4, Excelsior Brewery on slug

103

Aqua, 8.00", Top-Blob, Type-Blob, Bot-Smooth, R-5

SPRENGER, J. J.

101

Dark Green, 7.25", Top-Applied Top, Type-Squat, Bot-Iron Pontil, R-5, removed J.A. Sprengers initials from mold

102

Dark Green, 7.00", Top-Double-Taper, Type-Squat, Bot-Iron Pontil, R-5

103

Dark Green, 7.25", Top-Double-Taper, Type-Squat, Bot-Iron Pontil, R-5

SPRENGER, J.J. & J.A.

101-Front
Dark Green, 7.25", Top-Applied Top, Type-Iron Pontil, Bot-Iron Pontil, R-6

101-Rear
J.J. & J.A.S. initials on rear

102
Dark Green, 7.00", Top-Double-Taper, Type-Iron Pontil, Bot-Iron Pontil, R-6

SPRINGER, E. E. (Elizabeth)
Misspelled Springer should be Sprenger, please see E. E. Sprenger above.

SPRINGER, NELSON

101
Amber, 9.50, Top-Crown, Type-Crown, Bot-Smooth, R-6

102
Amber, 7.00, Top-Crown, Type-Crown, Bot-Smooth, R-6

STAR BOTTLING COMPANY

101

Aqua, 9.25", Top-Blob,
Type-Blob, Bot-Smooth,
R-5, large star on slug

STAR BOTTLING WORKS

101

Clear, 7.50", Top-Blob,
Type-Hutch, Bot-Smooth,
R-3, panel base

102

Clear, 9.00", Top-Crown,
Type-Soft Drink, Bot-
Smooth, R-1

103

Clear, 7.75", Top-Crown,
Type-Soft Drink, Bot-
Smooth, R-2

STAR BOTTLING WORKS - Continued

104

Aqua, 8.50", Top-Crown, Type-Soft Drink, Bot-Smooth, R-1

105

Apple Green, 7.75", Top-Crown, Type-Soft Drink, Bot-Smooth, R-2

106

Clear, 8.00", Top-Crown, Type-Soft Drink, Bot-Smooth, R-1

107

Clear, 11.00", Top-Crown, Type-Soft Drink, Bot-Smooth, R-1, nothing in slug plate, contents and registered embossing

STAR BREWING & BOTTLING WORKS

101

Aqua, 9.25", Top-Blob, Type-Blob, Bot-Smooth, R-5,
only Lancaster bottle with a Jewish "Star of David"

SUNCREST BOTTLING COMPANY

Please see Dr. Pepper Bottling Company above.

TODD, HARRY

101

Honey Amber, 7.75", Top-Blob, Type-Pony, Bot-Smooth, R-6

102

Clear, 9.00", Top-Blob, Type-Blob, Bot-Smooth, R-4

TRETTER, JOHN N.

101

Aqua, 6.50", Top-Blob, Type-Hutch, Bot-Smooth, R-2, medium horseshoe

102

Aqua, 6.50", Top-Blob, Type-Hutch, Bot-Smooth, R-3, JNO for John, medium horseshoe

103

Clear, 6.50", Top-Blob, Type-Hutch, Bot-Smooth, R-2, medium horseshoe

104

Aqua, 9.00", Top-Blob, Type-Blob, Bot-Smooth, R-1, medium horseshoe

105

Aqua, 9.50", Top-Blob, Type-Blob, Bot-Smooth, R-2, large horseshoe

106

Aqua, 9.00", Top-Blob, Type-Blob, Bot-Smooth, R-2, small horseshoe

TRETTER, JOHN N. - Continued

107

Aqua, 9.25", Top-Blob, Type-Blob, Bot-Smooth, R-1, medium horseshoe, lady leg neck, panel base

108

Clear, 9.25", Top-Blob, Type-Blob, Bot-Smooth, R-4, small type size

109

Clear, 9.25", Top-Blob, Type-Blob, Bot-Smooth, R-1, large shield, registered above shield

110

Clear, 9.50", Top-Blob, Type-Blob, Bot-Smooth, R-1, large shield

111

Clear, 9.25", Top-Blob, Type-Blob, Bot-Smooth, R-1, large shield, registered on shoulder

TRETTER, JOHN N. & SONS

101

Aqua, 6.00", Top-Blob,
Type-Hutch, Bot-Smooth,
R-1

102

Clear, 6.50", Top-Blob,
Type-Hutch, Bot-Smooth,
R-2

103

Clear, 6.75", Top-Blob,
Type-Hutch, Bot-Smooth,
R-3, panel base

104

Clear, 6.75", Top-Crown,
Type-Crown, Bot-Smooth,
R-4, panel base

ULMER, H. W. (Hiram)

101
Aqua, 9.00", Top-Blob, Type-Blob, Bot-Smooth, R-3

102
Clear, 9.25", Top-Blob, Type-Blob, Bot-Smooth, R-3

103
Clear, 9.25", Top-Blob, Type-Blob, Bot-Smooth, R-5, no capacity on rear of bottle

104
Clear, 9.25", Top-Crown, Type-Crown, Bot-Smooth, R-3

WACKER BREWING COMPANY (OLD)

101

Med Green, 7.25, Top-Applied Top, Type-Squat, Bot-Iron Pontil, R-7, unique, found in the original walls of the Wacker Brewery, during the renovation to become AA Electric.

WACKER BREWING COMPANY (NEW)

101

Aqua, 8.75", Top-Crown, Type-Crown, Bot-Smooth, R-2, darker color

102

Aqua, 8.75", Top-Crown, Type-Crown, Bot-Smooth, R-1

103

Aqua, 8.75", Top-Crown, Type-Crown, Bot-Smooth, R-2, states Brewery not Brewing

104

Aqua, 7.75", Top-Crown, Type-Crown, Bot-Smooth, R-1

105

Aqua, 7.75", Top-Crown, Type-Crown, Bot-Smooth, R-1

106

Amber, 7.00, Top-Crown, Type-Crown, Bot-Smooth, R-5

WACKER BREWING COMPANY (NEW) - Continued

107

Amber, 7.00, Top-Crown, Type-Crown, Bot-Smooth, R-1, Int Rev Tax paid

108

Amber, 9.75, Top-Crown, Type-Crown, Bot-Smooth, R-1

109

Amber, 9.50, Top-Crown, Type-Crown, Bot-Smooth, R-1

110

Amber, 9.75, Top-Crown, Type-Crown, Bot-Smooth, R-2

111

Amber, 6.75, Top-Crown, Type-Crown, Bot-Smooth, R-3

112

Amber, 6.75, Top-Crown, Type-Crown, Bot-Smooth, R-3

WACKER BREWING COMPANY (NEW) - Continued

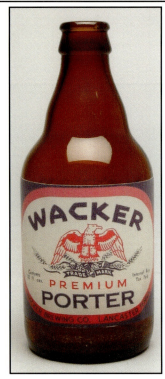

113

Amber, 7.00, Top-Crown, Type-Crown, Bot-Smooth, R-2, contents on left side of label

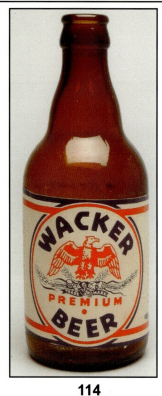

114

Amber, 7.00, Top-Crown, Type-Crown, Bot-Smooth, R-2, states 12 Fl. oz

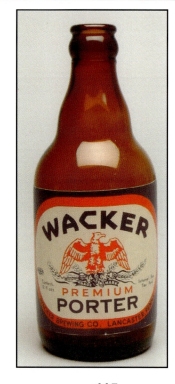

115

Amber, 7.00, Top-Crown, Type-Crown, Bot-Smooth, R-2, stamp left side of label

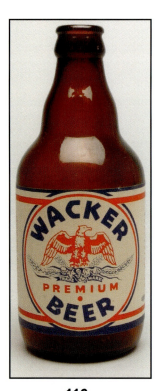

116

Amber, 7.00, Top-Crown, Type-Crown, Bot-Smooth, R-2, mislabeled one quart

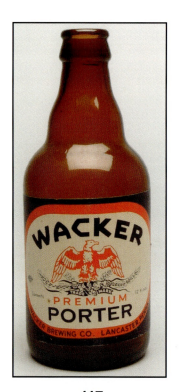

117

Amber, 7.00, Top-Crown, Type-Crown, Bot-Smooth, R-2, stamp left side of label

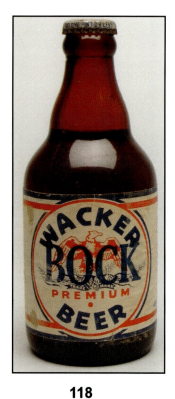

118

Amber, 7.00, Top-Crown, Type-Crown, Bot-Smooth, R-3

WACKER BREWING COMPANY (NEW) - Continued

119

Amber, 7.00, Top-Crown,
Type-Crown, Bot-Smooth,
R-3

120

Amber, 7.00, Top-Crown,
Type-Crown, Bot-Smooth,
R-1

121

Amber, 7.00, Top-Crown,
Type-Crown, Bot-Smooth,
R-1

122

Amber, 7.00, Top-Crown,
Type-Crown, Bot-Smooth,
R-1

123

Amber, 7.00, Top-Crown,
Type-Crown, Bot-Smooth,
R-2

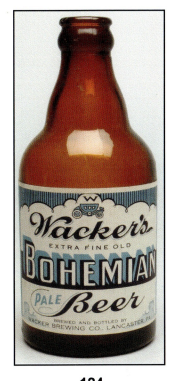

124

Amber, 7.00, Top-Crown,
Type-Crown, Bot-Smooth,
R-2

WACKER BREWING COMPANY (NEW) - Continued

125

Amber, 9.75, Top-Crown, Type-Crown, Bot-Smooth, R-2

126

Amber, 9.50, Top-Crown, Type-Crown, Bot-Smooth, R-1

127

Amber, 7.00, Top-Crown, Type-Crown, Bot-Smooth, R-1

128

Amber, 9.75, Top-Crown, Type-Crown, Bot-Smooth, R-2

129

Amber, 6.75, Top-Crown, Type-Crown, Bot-Smooth, R-2, pyro, contents

130

Amber, 7.00, Top-Crown, Type-Crown, Bot-Smooth, R-1, pyro

WACKER BREWING COMPANY (NEW) - Continued

131

Amber, 7.00, Top-Crown, Type-Crown, Bot-Smooth, R-6

132

Amber, 7.00, Top-Crown, Type-Crown, Bot-Smooth, R-6

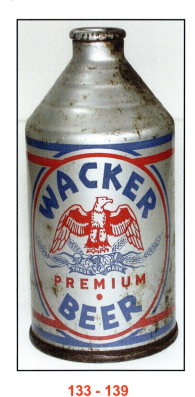

133 - 139

Tin, 5.00, Top-Crown, Type-Crowntainer, Bot-Smooth, R-6, very desirable, 7 variants exist from 5" to quart

WACKER BROS.

101

Aqua, 9.25", Top-Blob, Type-Blob, Bot-Smooth, R-4

102

Aqua, 9.50", Top-Blob, Type-Blob, Bot-Smooth, R-1, panel base

103

Aqua, 9.50", Top-Blob, Type-Blob, Bot-Smooth, R-1, panel base

WACKER BROS. - Continued

104

Aqua, 9.50", Top-Blob,
Type-Blob, Bot-Smooth,
R-1, panel base

105

Aqua, 8.75", Top-Blob,
Type-Blob, Bot-Smooth,
R-2

106

Aqua, 9.50", Top-Crown,
Type-Crown, Bot-Smooth,
R-1, panel base

107

Aqua, 9.50", Top-Crown,
Type-Crown, Bot-Smooth,
R-1

108

Aqua, 9.25", Top-Crown,
Type-Crown, Bot-Smooth,
R-1

WACKER BROS. - Continued

109

Clear, 9.00", Top-Crown, Type-Crown, Bot-Smooth, R-1

110

Modern Green, 9.50, Top-Crown, Type-Crown, Bot-Smooth, R-5

WACKER, JOSEPH

101

Dark Green, 7.00", Top-Double-Taper, Type-Squat, Bot-Smooth, R-5

102

Med Green, 7.00", Top-Double-Taper, Type-Squat, Bot-Smooth, R-5

103

Aqua, 7.50", Top-Applied Top, Type-Squat, Bot-Smooth, R-4

WALKER, THOMAS

101

Aqua, 7.00", Top-Double-Taper, Type-Squat, Bot-Smooth, R-5

102

Aqua, 7.00", Top-Applied Top, Type-Squat, Bot-Iron Pontil, R-5

103

Apple Green, 7.00", Top-Applied Top, Type-Squat, Bot-Iron Pontil, R-7, unique

WALL, GEORGE

101

Aqua, 9.50", Top-Blob, Type-Blob, Bot-Smooth, R-4

151

WANBAUGH & HAINES

101 - Front

Aqua, 6.75", Top-Blob, Type-Hutch, Bot-Smooth, R-6

102

Aqua, 9.25", Top-Blob, Type-Blob, Bot-Smooth, R-5

Neck label for Lebanon Brewing Company Beer, R-6, both Wanbaugh and Haines misspelled

WARE, E. C. (Ephraim)

101-Front

Dark Green, 6.75", Top-Double-Taper, Type-Squat, Bot-Iron Pontil, R-5,

101-106-Rear

Union Glass Works Philadelphia, Brown Stout

102

Dark Green, 7.75", Top-Applied Top, Type-Squat, Bot-Iron Pontil, R-6, WBE Ware Bottling Enterprise

WARE, E. C. (Ephraim) - Continued

103
Med Green, 7.50", Top-Applied Top, Type-Squat, Bot-Iron Pontil, R-4

104
Med Green, 6.75", Top-Double-Taper, Type-Squat, Bot-Iron Pontil, R-4

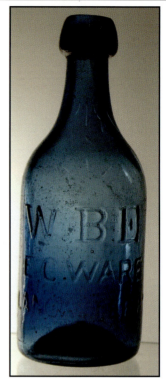
105
Cobalt Blue, 7.75", Top-Applied Top, Type-Squat, Bot-Iron Pontil, R-7. This is the rarest Lancaster bottle.

WARE, E. C. (Ephraim) - Cont.   WEBER, GEORGE

106-Front
Aqua, 6.75", Top-Double-Taper, Type-Squat, Bot-Iron Pontil, R-6, Large W.B.E. slug plate, Ware Bottling Enterprise

101
Aqua, 6.25", Top-Blob, Type-Hutch, Bot-Smooth, R-2, horseshoe facing up

102
Aqua, 6.50", Top-Blob, Type-Hutch, Bot-Smooth, R-1, small horseshoe

WEBER, GEORGE - Continued

103
Aqua, 6.25", Top-Blob, Type-Hutch, Bot-Smooth, R-2, horseshoe facing up

104
Aqua, 7.25, Top-Blob, Type-Pony, Bot-Smooth, R-4, horseshoe facing up

105
Aqua, 9.00, Top-Blob, Type-Blob, Bot-Smooth, R-4, horseshoe facing up

WEBER, GEORGE - Cont.   WHISTLE BOTTLING CO.

106
Aqua, 9.25, Top-Blob, Type-Blob, Bot-Smooth, R-4, medium horseshoe

107
Aqua, 9.25, Top-Blob, Type-Blob, Bot-Smooth, R-5, medium horseshoe, no embossing on rear

101
Aqua, 7.50", Top-Crown, Type-Crown, Bot-Smooth, R-1

WHISTLE BOTTLING CO. - Continued

102

Clear, 7.50", Top-Crown, Type-Soft Drink, Bot-Smooth, R-1

103

Clear, 7.50", Top-Crown, Type-Soft Drink, Bot-Smooth, R-1, Crackle Finish, K same as W W Keefer # 109, Lettering diagonal along bottle

WHISTLE BOTTLING CO. - Continued   WILEY, MYERS E.

104

Clear, 7.50", Top-Crown, Type-Soft Drink, Bot-Smooth, R-1, Hourglass figure, Lancaster, PA on bottom, Patent Date of 1926

105

Clear, 7.50", Top-Crown, Type-Soft Drink, Bot-Smooth, R-1

101

Clear, 9.00", Top-Blob, Type-Blob, Bot-Smooth, R-5, MEW on Slug Plate

WOLPERT, PETER K.

101

Clear, 9.25", Top-Blob,
Type-Blob, Bot-Smooth,
R-5

102

Clear, 9.25", Top-Blob,
Type-Blob, Bot-Smooth,
R-6, registered on neck

ZECH, CHAS. (Charles)

101

Aqua, 6.75", Top-Blob,
Type-Hutch, Bot-Smooth,
R-5, states Brewery

102

Aqua, 7.00", Top-Blob,
Type-Hutch, Bot-Smooth,
R-1

103

Aqua, 6.75", Top-Blob,
Type-Hutch, Bot-Smooth,
R-1

ZECH, CHAS. (Charles) - Continued

104

Clear, 6.50", Top-Blob, Type-Hutch, Bot-Smooth, R-2, Zech on bottom

105

Clear, 6.50", Top-Blob, Type-Hutch, Bot-Smooth, R-1

106

Apple Green, 6.75", Top-Blob, Type-Hutch, Bot-Smooth, R-2

107

Aqua, 6.50", Top-Blob, Type-Hutch, Bot-Smooth, R-1, panel base

108

Clear, 7.00", Top-Blob, Type-Hutch, Bot-Smooth, R-1

109

Aqua, 6.50", Top-Blob, Type-Hutch, Bot-Smooth, R-2, Bottler

ZECH, CHAS. (Charles) - Continued

110

Aqua, 7.75", Top-Blob, Type-Small Blob, Bot-Smooth, R-3

111

Aqua, 9.25", Top-Blob, Type-Blob, Bot-Smooth, R-6, Zech misspelled as Zeck

112

Aqua, 9.25", Top-Blob, Type-Blob, Bot-Smooth, R-1

113

Aqua, 6.50", Top-Blob, Type-Blob, Bot-Smooth, R-2, states Bottling Works

114

Clear, 6.50", Top-Blob, Type-Blob, Bot-Smooth, R-3, states Bottler

115

Aqua, 8.75", Top-Blob, Type-Blob, Bot-Smooth, R-1

ZECH, CHAS. (Charles) - Continued

116

Aqua, 9.50", Top-Blob, Type-Blob, Bot-Smooth, R-1

117

Aqua, 9.00", Top-Blob, Type-Blob, Bot-Smooth, R-1

118

Aqua, 9.50", Top-Blob, Type-Blob, Bot-Smooth, R-1, This Bottle Never Sold

119

Clear, 9.75", Top-Blob, Type-Blob, Bot-Smooth, R-1

120

Aqua, 9.75", Top-Blob, Type-Blob, Bot-Smooth, R-1, panel base

121

Clear, 9.75", Top-Crown, Type-Crown, Bot-Smooth, R-1, states Bottler

ZECH, CHAS. (Charles) - Continued

122

Honey Amber, 9.50", Top-Crown, Type-Crown, Bot-Smooth, R-6, extremely rare color

123

Aqua, 8.00", Top-Crown, Type-Crown, Bot-Smooth, R-1

124

Aqua, 8.00", Top-Crown, Type-Crown, Bot-Smooth, R-2

125

Clear, 7.75", Top-Crown, Type-Crown, Bot-Smooth, R-1

126

Clear, 8.25", Top-Crown, Type-Crown, Bot-Smooth, R-1

127

Clear, 8.00", Top-Crown, Type-Crown, Bot-Smooth, R-1

ZECH, CHAS. (Charles) - Continued

128

Aqua, 7.75", Top-Crown, Type-Crown, Bot-Smooth, R-1

129

Clear, 8.00", Top-Crown, Type-Crown, Bot-Smooth, R-1

130

Clear, 8.00", Top-Crown, Type-Crown, Bot-Smooth, R-1

131

Aqua, 7.75", Top-Crown, Type-Crown, Bot-Smooth, R-1

132

Aqua, 7.75", Top-Crown, Type-Crown, Bot-Smooth, R-5, Zech misspelled as Zeck

133

Aqua, 7.75", Top-Crown, Type-Crown, Bot-Smooth, R-2, states Bottling

ZECH, CHAS. (Charles) - Continued

134

Clear, 8.25", Top-Crown, Type-Crown, Bot-Smooth, R-1, icicles

135

Clear, 8.00", Top-Crown, Type-Crown, Bot-Smooth, R-1, icicles

136-Front

Amber, 7.50", Top-Crown, Type-Crown, Bot-Smooth, R-1, crackle surface

136-Bottom

137

Aqua, 7.50", Top-Crown, Type-Crown, Bot-Smooth, R-2

138

Aqua, 6.75", Top-Blob, Type-Hutch, Bot-Smooth, R-3

139

Aqua, 7.50", Top-Crown, Type-Crown, Bot-Smooth, R-2

NOTES

NOTES

ABOUT THE AUTHORS

John Long

John, born in Lancaster, is a J. P. McCaskey High School Alumnus. Later, he received a B.S. degree from Millersville State Teachers College with a major in Industrial Arts Education. In 1962, John was presented a Masters in Education diploma as a member of the first graduating advanced degree class of Millersville University, PA. Most of John's 34 years of teaching were at his old high school where he instructed many Industrial Arts courses including: Graphic Arts and Photography. Married to Carol Ressler Long, they have two children and four granddaughters.

John's interest in antiques and craftsmanship was cultivated by his college studies. He received his first Lancaster brewery bottles when a colleague gave him several old bottles as a "thank you" for his help in assisting his friend with the disposal of some inherited possessions.

Sam Nolt

Sam, a Lancaster, Pennsylvania native, was also graduated by J. P. McCaskey High School and then Franklin and Marshall College. As a business and history major, he completed college in 1960. After serving two years in the US Army, he returned to Lancaster as a salesman for J. L. Clark Manufacturing Company (now Clarcor). After many years, Sam was promoted to Manager of National Accounts. He traveled for business throughout the United States, and retired in the year 2001. Married for over 45 years to Joyce Weaver Nolt, his high school sweetheart, Sam is the father of two grown children, Tim and Kristin, and grandfather to three preschoolers.

Sam began his bottle collecting with his first Lancaster bottle purchase in the late 1960's. He paid $0.50 for this find at a Cherry Hill, New Jersey mall, during a sales trip lunch hour. He continues to improve his accumulation of Lancaster, Pennsylvania items even today, after some forty years with the collecting fever.

Curt Tomlinson

Curt is a Lancaster native and he too was graduated, in 1978, by J. P. McCaskey High School. Coincidently, one of his fellow authors, John Long was Curt's teacher, and was instrumental in mentoring Curt toward pursuing a college education. Curt was graduated by Millersville University, in 1982, with a B.S. degree in Industrial Arts.

Curt worked many years in the computer field. In 1994, Curt quit his job to open his own business. With two children and one on the way, Curt started GNet, an Internet development firm in his basement. Curt sold GNet in 1999 and finally went into semi-retirement in 2001. In 2002, Curt started his next business venture Seisan, an LBS mapping development firm.

Curt has been married to his wife Ronda Lyter Tomlinson for 23 years. They have three children: Nathan, Megan and Lauren. Curt enjoys hunting, fishing and privy digging. In any given week, one can find Curt dressed in a suit or knee-deep in mud in a local privy pit.